A POT FROM SHARDS

A POT FROM SHARDS

Joan Wexler

IPBOOKS.net
International Psychoanalytic Books

New York • http://www.IPBooks.net

Published by International Psychoanalytic Books (IPBooks)
Queens, NY
Online at www.IPBooks.net

DISCLAIMER
This book is a memoir. It reflects the author's personal recollections of experiences over time. Some names have been changed, some events have been compressed, and dialogues have been re-created.

Book design and formatting services by Self-Publishing Lab

Front cover design by Kathy Kovacic, BlackthornStudio.com

ISBN: 978-1-949093-32-2

For Harry
A Love Story

Contents

PART III
JOINING THE WORLD—COMINGS AND GOINGS

CONTENTS

Part IV
Damage and Repair

TIMELINE

Memory often ignores linear time operating more by association of themes and feelings across time. This can be confusing for a reader or listener. Following is a brief timeline to orient the reader when necessary.

1938	Born in New York City.
1940	My mother leaves my father. She and I move in with my grandmother and aunt.
1943	My grandmother becomes my primary caretaker.
1943–1948	Many trips between Miami and New York with many schools and apartment changes. Sometimes my grandmother and I are alone together, and sometimes my mother and aunt are with us.
1948	New York City—My mother marries her second husband, Irv. I leave my grandmother's care to live with my mother and Irv.
1950–1956	My mother divorces Irv, and she and I continue to live alone together in New York. I begin to seriously study dance and attend the High School of Performing Arts.

TIMELINE

1955–1956	I dance professionally with a New York City dance company
1956–1960	College
1960	Harry and I marry and live in Connecticut
1964	My mother marries for the third time
1964	Degree in Clinical Social Work and practice of psychotherapy
1967	Our son Matthew is born.
1970	Our daughter Sarah is born.
1970	My father dies although I don't learn this until 2008.
1978	My grandmother dies.
1998	Graduate from a psychoanalytic institute
1999	First granddaughter born
2002	First grandson born
2002	Aunt's death
2003	Mother's death
2005	Second granddaughter born
2018	Harry's death

PART I

SHAPING THE POT

When a parent goes missing how do we shape and fill the empty space?

For the listener, who listens in the snow,
And, nothing himself, beholds
Nothing that is not there and the nothing that is.
Wallace Stevens—The Snow Man

June 2008: Death Certificate

In June 2008, I logged on-line the name of my long-missing father who I barely knew. This time something came onto the screen I had never seen before, a blurry facsimile of his death certificate. Some of it was legible. I could read that he died in San Francisco in 1970 at age sixty-one. That was a complete surprise. I never imagined him in California, and I didn't know when he died. There was clearly more information on the screen image, but I couldn't make it out. Writing to the California Board of Health I requested a paper copy. They needed to know my relationship to the deceased. Writing in the word daughter in relation to my father was a unique experience. The paper certificate soon arrived and recorded his birth as December 1908 in New York City and his profession as actor. I already knew this information about him, so I was reassured this was the right person. His name was John Pote. I had come to believe that the only thing I had of him or from him was his name.

My mother left my father in 1940 when I was two years old. She and I continued to live in New York. There were a few visits with him that I can still remember. All visits stopped early in 1943 when I was about five. Then all contact with him ended. There were no letters, no birthday cards, no photographs, and no child support. A few years later when my mother legally divorced him, I heard from her that he moved out of New York City to live with his mother in Westchester County. In 1959, when I was a senior in college, I looked for and found his name in a Westchester phone book. I called him, and we met once, then nothing again until 2008 when I came upon his death certificate. Everything on the document other than the date of his birth and his profession was a surprise.

Suddenly I owned more than his name.

The cause of death is listed as "cirrhosis of the liver, chronic alcoholism, and heart failure." I knew, from my mother that he drank heavily. The certificate also notes that the day before he died he was a patient at San Francisco General Hospital. His listed spouse is "Florence-maiden name unknown." Why didn't he know Florence's maiden name? Now that I knew her first name I could search further. Ancestry.com revealed Florence Pote to be my father's third wife. My mother, Marion, was his second wife. I knew he had been married before he married my mother. On-line census information revealed that at the time of John Pote's death, Florence Pote lived in Modesto, California and had already lived there for several years. They must have been separated. I also learn that Florence Pote was ten years older than my father. She died in Modesto, California in 1980 and John Pote is recorded as her husband. They may have been separated, but they were not divorced.

Looking online at both the New York and California census information reveals he left New York in 1963 and moved to San Francisco.

Also appearing on the death certificate is an unexplained number and letter code from the San Francisco General Hospital. I called the hospital to learn the code indicates that the patient agreed that on his death his body is to be donated to The University of California Medical

School to be used as a cadaver for medical students; to be dissected and the remains later cremated. Was there ever a funeral?

Although I barely knew him it still is startling to imagine my father's body as a picked over nameless cadaver on some young medical students dissecting table. But I can also call up Rembrandt's "The Anatomy Lesson of Dr. Nicolaes Tulp" and shift to a state of cold objectivity as I view that blue-white dead body. But maybe my father thought he was being useful or that he was giving himself as a gift. Or maybe he was utterly alone, and it was the only way he knew how to dispose of his own body.

The certificate gives the date and time of his death as October 11, 1970, at 10: pm. His address is 1082 Post Street, apartment number two.

Who was my father, John Pote? How did his brief presence and his long absence shape me? Does it still shape me? These are the questions behind all the major decisions of my life. Who do I love? Who do I avoid loving? What work should I do? What makes a life worth living or not worth living?

I decide to go to San Francisco, find his apartment building and explore his neighborhood. What more will I find?

August 2008: San Francisco Reflection

It is a chilly August morning in San Francisco. I'm glad I brought along a warm, red, zip-up sweater. I leave the hotel on Market Street to take a short walk to Post Street. The Google map shows 1082 to be close to the corner of Polk Street. Walking steeply uphill on Post while looking for number 1082 I see a sign on an old hotel, "The Saratoga," saying "Founded in 1908". I feel encouraged. 1908 is the year of my father's birth. It seems to speak to me saying, "Come along, you are on the right path now." Did he choose to live at Post and Polk because his name was Pote? As an actor I can imagine him declaiming in a loud resonant voice, "It's me Pote of Post and Polk!"

This neighborhood, known as The Tenderloin, is run-down and seedy with many cheap hotels, bars, and convenience stores. The Internet describes The Tenderloin as having been an oasis for gay and transvestite men long before The Castro developed. Now here in The Tenderloin, homeless men lie, sit or prop themselves in doorways. Some drink from bottles in paper bags. This was my father's neighborhood. Everything is saturated with meaning, signs, symbols, and hints about who he was. Am I prying uninvited into his secret world? Is he scowling at me?

At first, I walk all the way to the corner of Post and Polk Street. Without realizing it, I passed by and missed 1082. Here on the corner is the Lush Lounge. It is around 10:30 in the morning and I can see through the window several figures already huddling at the bar. The scene is like Hopper's painting "Night Café". People sit at a distance, some staring blankly—loneliness made visible. I backtrack on Post and find 1082. Directly across the street from 1082 is "The Diva", a well-known transvestite club described on the Internet.

1082 Post Street is an old, five-story, pale yellow apartment building. Zigzagging across the entire face of it is a fire escape. The locked front door is made of thick glass. Inside, a small vestibule holds rows of mailboxes. In front of the locked glass entrance door, I take photos of the building then bring the film to a drugstore with "1 Hour Photo Developing". While waiting I walk around the neighborhood. On the streets, except for a few young people who look like students, people seem poor. Some are old and disabled.

Back at the drugstore, I open the film packet and take out the first glossy picture showing the front of the apartment building. Stunned, I see myself in the photo wearing the red sweater. Captured in the reflection of the heavy glass door of the building is my image taking the photograph. It is merely my reflection, but I appear to be inside the building. I am looking inside—but I don't find my father—I find myself. Who is inside? Who is outside? Was I ever inside my father's mind? Did he ever think about me? This accidental photo trick catches my fantasy that I am a part of his interior. It brings home one of the very few available facts. While I may never have been in John's interior, he is vividly in mine.

Suddenly I am thinking "John," not "my father." Why? My mother only referred to him as "John," never as "your father". Perhaps I loosen his presence as "my father" with the hard-edged possibility, even likelihood that his absence from my life suggests he infrequently, if ever, thought about me. All the information I found never confirms he was my biological father. Except for his name on my birth certificate, nowhere does he list me as his kin, not on any marriage, divorce or census records that I could find. This is the first time I consider the possibility that he never tried to contact me because I was in fact not his child. By searching the Internet and finding his death certificate I seem to grant him a life and death of his own, separate from what I ever imagined his life to be.

As I hold this photograph of myself in his interior, this photograph of his existence in my mind, I realize I will never, ever know if he thought of me. All my images of John are my innumerable reflections based on what I heard from my mother, and our very few relatives, her brother and sister, and their mother, (my uncle, aunt and grandmother). I have no siblings or first cousins. I know no one else who knew John. There are no signs and symbols that will explain his life or what I may or may not have meant to him. I have only guesses and questions.

As John was slowly dying in San Francisco did his heart condition make it difficult for him to walk up the Post Street Hill? Did he desire men? There were strong hints he did. According to my mother, he often left their apartment at night wearing "stage-makeup" and went to McSorley's Tavern. McSorley's was a bar located in New York's Bowery and reserved for men only. But it was not necessarily known as a gay bar. There, he sang funny songs or recited Shakespeare. He was rewarded with drinks and applause—probably in need of both. My mother also said, on occasion, she dressed up to look like a young boy and they went to McSorley's together. There is another story told by my aunt, Natalia, my mother's sister. The two of them walked into the apartment and found John in bed with a man, so maybe he was gay. Perhaps living in early and mid-century America, being gay is what tormented him. Here in San Francisco did he find a place of solace? Here in the Tenderloin did he find kindred spirits at The Diva club and the Lush Lounge? Did he drink at the Lush Lounge? What did he think about? What did he feel? What did he worry about? What was the building at 1082 Post Street like when he lived there? Was it a respectable apartment building? Was it a single room occupancy? Did he live in a single room while his wife escaped to Modesto maybe paying his rent to ease her guilt for leaving him? Or, perhaps he left her. Before he died did he want to live in a place where being gay was more acceptable? Did he know no one would bury him and is that why he agreed to become a medical cadaver? Who found his dead body? Did anyone call Florence? Did she identify the body?

All these questions are impossible to answer. What purpose do they serve? Momentarily the questions give shape or an image, albeit fleeting to this elusive man who supposedly was my father. I need a shape. Otherwise, he is an abstraction.

Many years ago while turning over the pages of an issue of Smithsonian magazine I came upon a photograph of an ancient broken pot carefully reconstructed from a few connected shards. Against a dark background, it was lit from the inside revealing the few remaining actual pieces and the shapes of the pieces that were once there but were now missing. It was a photograph of the shapes of emptiness or absence. The image invited me to imagine the pot before its destruction. A whole pot revealed from a few shards is how I now hold in mind an image of my father—more missing than present, fragile and broken. The word pot is like a broken piece of his name, Pote.

Because there were no photographs, as a child I didn't know what he looked like except for my very vague memories. Carefully, I removed the page with the photograph from the magazine and framed it. It became a portrait of broken John Pot.

My preoccupation with John Pot(e) and all my questions offer ways to imagine this shape-shifting Pote/pot. Each brief shape feels like a moment of coherence, or pain, or fury or sympathy; a moment of condemnation or of understanding; sometimes even a moment of affection as I remember him during the rare visitations, reading to me or playing with me the way fathers play with their small children. But very soon the shape shifts. What do I gain? I gain a sense of John alive. I imagine him moving through his various landscapes in New York and now in San Francisco. As I imagine him living his life, I don't deaden his existence or a part of my own. Questions, thoughts, dreams, memories, and imaginings make a bridge that crosses the abyss of absence and emptiness reaching and quickening the John I hold in mind. I can love him or hate him or just be interested in him. It is as close as I can get to feeling the presence of a father, even if the father I imagine/create is not John or not who John was. These constantly shifting questions, paradoxically anchor his image into a pot or a collage, or perhaps just a crazy quilt of loose associations.

Memory and Hearsay

My mother told me that John Pote was an actor and playwright whose severe alcoholism soon thwarted any success he might have had. She left him, taking me with her when I was two years old. I occasionally met with him until I was four. I remember these visits. Soon all contact with John stopped. I don't know who made the decision, but I suspect it was my mother. As far as I know, he did not contest it.

My mother grew up without her father, and my grandmother grew up without her father. History repeated itself three times.

Some hazy memories of him, as well as stories told by family members, were tantalizing. But only his name felt like mine. The two sounds John and Pote were rarely far from my mind. Pote rhymes with coat. I used the sounds, rhymes, and parts of his name to play with him, to talk to him, to taunt him, to demean him and to elevate him. In my teens, I taunted him in fantasy with "imPOTEnt" expressing my anger at his absolute absence and what I imagined as his impotence to protest against my mother eliminating him from our lives. But I also needed to elevate him, to give him status and so he became "Pater OmniPOTEns".

While partially sarcastic it also spoke to my preoccupation and longing for a father.

Sometimes when people saw Pote written, they thought Pote might be pronounced Poté or maybe "potty." If I thought of John Pote as "the john" or "potty," I demeaned him capturing my mother's elimination of him and my grandmother's disgust, "…that drunken, lazy sponge." But for me "the john" and "potty", the bathroom and the toilet, were the places I returned to several times a day like other children might meet up with their fathers several times a day. Gentler moments, remembering he was an actor and writer, led me to transpose the e in his name making it poet. Preoccupation with the sounds, meanings, and parts of his name was urgent because I could not remember his face. I asked my mother why there were no pictures. She claimed she didn't know. I suspect there once were photographs, after all, he was an actor. Did he take his pictures with him? Were they destroyed? If so, who destroyed them?

When I look at the photograph of the ancient, broken pot, it feels charged with a compressed visual creation of my father, his existence and his destruction. I know that memory is unreliable; hearsay reveals more about the speaker than who is spoken about and even documented facts can be wrong. However, as I try to reconstruct this Pote/pot, I keep in mind that I am working with fragile, metaphorical clay, not solid stuff.

Insubstantial stuff also reminds me of Wallace Steven's poem "The Snowman"[1]

A Snowman is merely water. He will melt, evaporate, and disappear. Stevens coldly captures absent presence and present absence with, "Nothing that is not there and the nothing that is." The image of the

---

1 Stevens, Wallace. "The Snow Man." The Collected Poems of Wallace Stevens. Alfred A. Knopf, New York, 1954

broken pot, its present absence, and its absent presence brings to mind Steven's haunting line.

As a teenager and young adult curiosity about John Pote led me first, like him, into a performing profession. I became a modern dancer, performing in New York and always imagining, with both hope and trepidation, he might as a performing artist himself find dance of interest and be in the audience. I left dancing professionally soon after I began college. I could see that few dancers were able to sustain the relentless demands of a career in dance and an intact family life as well. I realized I wanted a normal life, a life with a man who shows-up and stays and I wanted children, even more than I wanted to dance. I married at age twenty-one and became a clinical social worker and psychotherapist. Later, I trained as a psychoanalyst. I wanted structure, meaning, and constancy. This was revolutionary in the family I was born into.

During the early, brief periods of visitations with John, when I was between the ages of two and four, we met in the minister's study in St. Thomas Church in New York where I attended nursery school. I have a vision of his solid form sitting in a large leather chair. I have no image of his face. I stand leaning against the arm of the chair while he reads me a story. I imagine the story is, James Thurber's "Many Moons"—the story of a king desperately worried about his young daughter. Shaded lamps dimly light the minister's study and reflect warmly off mahogany wainscoting. I remember John playing with me in a rough and tumble way, hanging me upside down. Apparently, I screamed. Was I scared? Was I thrilled? Probably both. I suspect it was a new experience. I don't think any other man played with me in such an exciting way. On hearing my screams, I remember my mother, who waited outside the door charge in, her face contorted in rage and yelling, "Stop it, stop it! She's too little, you can't do that." Was she furious with him for handling me roughly? That was the last visit. My mother gained full custody.

My father contributed no financial support—he may well have been unable to do so. He did not call or send birthday cards or presents. He disappeared. Today, if he indeed were my father, he would be called a "deadbeat dad".

Another memory—when I was thirteen and preparing to audition for New York's High School of Performing Arts, my dance teacher, Erick Hawkins, helped me to prepare a dance for the audition. He was a gentle man with whom I had always felt comfortable. He had shown an interest in me and went out of his way to telephone my mother occasionally to suggest dance concerts and museum exhibits that would benefit my dance training. I was old enough to wonder who he was more interested in, my mother or me but maybe both of us. Until the audition preparation, I had never been alone with him. I walked to his apartment, which was close to where we lived. There, he had a private studio where he worked on his own choreography. We set to work, and suddenly I felt panicky. He was well aware that something was wrong. I could not understand or explain my distress but said I suddenly didn't feel well and left. We made another time to meet. I went home, still unable to explain what was wrong but pleaded with my mother to come to these sessions with me and wait outside the door, which meant she had to sit on some cold steps in the building hallway. She, of course, asked me why but I didn't know why. She came and sat just outside the door. Soon Erick realized that she waited for me and he invited her in bringing a chair into the studio. Was I re-creating that frightening and thrilling moment when my father was vigorously playing with me—lifting me up and turning me upside down, (what fathers do) when my mother, waiting outside the door, came charging in screaming at him? Why now with Erick would I want to risk reliving that scene? Was it because it is my only memory of my mother and father together? Was I bringing Erick and my mother together? Maybe this time, with Erick, it would be different. Erick had recently been divorced, and my mother too had recently divorced her second husband. When Erick called and spoke to her I know, I harbored the fantasy that they would fall in love, marry and I would finally have a normal family. That didn't happen.

I went on to the High School of Performing Arts and moved on to work with other dancers and choreographers. Erick went on to fall in love with a woman in his company. I left studying with Erick, but from time to time we might meet by chance in the city or at a concert. I always went back-stage when he performed, and he always greeted me warmly. I think of him as a very important man in my life during a crucial time when I was leaving childhood and entering teenage. Even if I wondered who he was more interested in, my mother or me he was very generous toward me with his time and his support. He never had children. I hope by loving and admiring him as I did that I too brought something to his life at that time.

My mother, in spite of purging my father from our lives, did not purge him from her memory. She willingly talked about him, especially when we were on our frequent walks around New York or riding together on buses or subways. From her, I learned that in the 1920s and 30s he worked as an actor with The Works Progress Administration Theatre. The W.P.A. during the 1930s supported the best years of his work. He taught acting there and my mother, who wanted to be an actor, was one of his students. When the W.P.A. unraveled so did he. His drinking escalated to the point where he no longer functioned. She told me they had terrible screaming fights sometimes kicking and hitting each other.

She also thought he was very clever and witty and she sang to me the silly songs he liked to sing. One, an old Dutch children's song starts out, "In the walley in the vintertime ven the vind blow through the vindow panes…"

As I grew older I wanted more facts, like, "Did he go to college?" She told me he went to Oxford. She also told me his mother occasionally became psychotic and was hospitalized. At those times he apparently went to live with an aunt in Maine. Once, looking at a map of Maine, I noticed there is a region called Oxford and began to suspect that he may have attended a Maine elementary or high school that was called Oxford, not the University.

She seemed to know nothing about his father. I can imagine my mother as a young, starry-eyed, wannabe actress who was wooed by a handsome actor and wanted to believe all the glamorous things he had to say about himself. He described himself as a Shakespearian actor yet I have never found anything to suggest that he actually performed in a Shakespeare production.

He was married to his first wife, Renée when he met my mother. She, also an actor, was from Haiti. In the 1920 Census list, she records her race as "Negro." I have to admire my father for daring to marry out of his race in the 1930s. He divorced Renée and apparently proposed to my mother on her birthday while handing her his divorce papers wrapped as a birthday present. I heard they eloped and I was born two years later at a time when their lives together were dissolving. He constantly drank I heard, even needing a drink to get out of bed in the morning. Apparently, they fought about his drinking and his growing inability to work. I can imagine that a baby in the mix was too much. My mother said she knew she had to leave him. She moved out and soon moved into an apartment with her mother and sister.

Often, years later I would find her sobbing on her bed. Usually, her grief had to do with another doomed love affair she was having, but sometimes she would say, "I miss John". I believe she did love him, in spite of exiling him. I wonder if she might have stayed with him if I had not entered the scene.

When I imagine transposing the "e" in Pote and making it "poet", it fits some of my mother's descriptions of him. He called himself a playwright, yet she said he managed to write only the first act of plays. He never finished them. She thinks he sold them to other writers who finished them and then sold them as their own. Apparently, he had a sharp wit, could recite reams of Shakespeare and sang Noel Coward songs. When I imagine him singing and reciting at McSorley's, I picture him as Dylan Thomas, loud, lyrical, swollen and swaggering.

I was always on the lookout for information about John Pote. In crowded streets and places like theaters and railroad stations, I wondered if he was nearby. If I waited for a train at Grand Central Station, I went to their collection of nationwide phone books hoping to find his name. I found several people named Pote and wrote to them. The only connection I found who responded was a Catholic priest living in Brooklyn. He was distantly related. His mother was Catholic, and he was raised as a Catholic. He was about the same age as my father but never met him and knew nothing about the immediate family except that John was his parents' only child.

As time passed, the fathers' of my friends began to die. I attended their funerals. When I heard sons and daughters tell stories about their lives with their fathers I felt my father's absence with a new force. I imagined his death.

At that time I found, in a book of photographs, a picture of a man's black coat lying frozen and stiff in dirty snow. The image haunted me. Did a man wearing a black coat fall in the snow and die there? Is that how my father died in the Bowery after a night of drinking? Was John Pote in that stiff black coat? Was he alone, drunk and numb then stumbled in the snow? Did he give up and die? Where was the body? Did it shrivel to dust? Did it blow away in the winter wind? But where are the bones? Did he gather up his bones and walk? Does he roam the city? I never imagined him moving to San Francisco.

His disappearance, my longing and the mystery of who was my father make demands on my imagination to stay curious. What I imagine about him shapes me. But I also wanted facts.

With the arrival of the Internet, I continued to search. I used as my guide, Daniel Mendelsohn's book, The Lost[2] in which he uses the Internet to trace relatives lost in the Holocaust. Much earlier, because I had begun to wonder if John might be gay, I also read Mendelsohn's book *The Elusive Embrace*[3].

Along with Proust, it is the most vivid description of gay male desire I ever found.

I was soon able to find John Pote's name associated with the W.P.A. theatre and also found that in the early 1920s he had several small parts in Broadway plays. I found no information about his career after the 1930s. At first, I found two marriage certificates I knew about. The first dated 1930 is his marriage to Renée. That marriage ended in 1936 when he married Marion, my mother. John and Marion separated in 1940 and later divorced. After finding his death certificate and learning his third wife was Florence, I discovered that marriage certificate as well.

As disturbing as it was to learn the possible facts of my father's end, it was also in some ways strangely settling. It made him less elusive.

When I imagine him alone and sick signing onto the disposal of his body as a cadaver, I am sorrow-struck that this probably talented man had to arrive at the end of his life in such a desperate way. When I imagine his embalmed body invaded and dissected, my mind seeks the more aesthetic and disembodied image of shards from a broken pot.

---

2 Mendelsohn, Daniel. The Lost: A Search for Six of Six Million, Harper Collins, 2006

3 Mendelsohn, Daniel. The Elusive Embrace: Desire and the Riddle of Identity, Vintage paperback, 2000

"Shards" offers a balance of the objective and the painful, allowing me to hold and to contain, multiple thoughts and feelings at once, sad, horrified and dispassionate.

Throughout the trip to San Francisco, I kept in regular phone contact with Harry, my husband. The date of my trip was partly determined by our son Matthew's plan to attend a professional meeting in San Francisco at the same time. Later that day, after my first visit to John's apartment building, Matthew arrived. He immediately wanted to walk with me to Post Street to see the building and neighborhood. Of course, John never knew of Matthew's existence.

Matthew is adopted. Harry and I yearned for children. Harry, because he grew up with two siblings he is close to. Children were always a part of his life. His parents were teachers and also ran a summer camp. The hurly-burly of children and family is a part of why I was so attracted to Harry. I yearned for children because I hungrily looked for a family and wanted to create the normality I didn't have. I wanted more than one child because I wanted to create siblings and hoped they would create cousins. I found growing up with no siblings and no cousins lonely and unconnected.

I had three miscarriages, and still no baby came. My body felt empty, and our lives had unfilled space. Feeling empty was especially acute when we sat down to a meal. I had shared many meals with the families of my friends and with Harry's parents and his brother and sister. At meals families talk, complain, tell stories about friends and enemies, have arguments with each other all while eating. And if it is a working family they return for the next meal with pleasure or anger but they survive it and life goes on together. As they break bread together, they fill themselves with both nourishment and emotional connection.

After four years of trying to have a baby, we applied for adoption and remarkably nine months after we applied we received the call that we had our son. Matthew, born in 1967 is named for Harry's maternal grandfather Max who stayed with his wife and family and for my maternal grandfather Marvin who left, and my grandmother's father, Marek who also left.

When Matthew married he and his wife wished for children. Matthew for the first time felt a strong need to search for his birth mother, possibly to learn about his genetic pool, perhaps because his wish to create a new generation invited him to wonder about his origins. He found his birth mother through the records of the adoption agency. She greeted his call saying," I have been waiting for this call for thirty-two years." An empty space was filled. She is married with three children. Over time she and Matthew have worked out a friendly relationship. Her husband always knew she had given birth to Matthew. She welcomes Matthew's occasional calls. If he happens to be in the vicinity of her home, he may visit. From her, he learned a lot about his maternal inheritance, but she was reluctant to speak in any detail about Matthew's birth father. While Matthew grew up with a strong and loving adoptive father, biological paternity for him also remains mysterious.

In 1970, Harry and I adopted our daughter Sarah. Sarah is named for Harry's paternal grandmother Sarah. Names can signify life, continuity and in Jewish tradition also death but named in the book of life.

Recently, Sarah initiated a search for her own birth family. Sadly her birth mother died several years before, but her maternal aunt greeted Sarah's search with great warmth and a welcoming invitation to visit and to meet the extended family. Relatives shared many stories about her birth mother's life so Sarah was able to fill in some of the empty spaces about her origins. However, they knew nothing about Sarah's birth father.

Sarah married and in 1999 became pregnant. Together we watched many videos of childbirth. When Sarah was about to deliver, she asked me to be present at her baby's birth, saying, "Because you never actually gave birth, you need this experience Mom." For me, it was such an inclusive, loving and perceptive gift and so rooted in the reality of Sarah's adoption and my infertility. At 5:00 AM on November 3, 1999, exhilarated and amazed I watched our granddaughter's head crown. Sarah also gave me the privilege of cutting the cord. Then, an ordinary miracle occurred. The new baby girl turned from gray-white to pink, cried out announcing her arrival and was settled onto Sarah's chest. Sarah greeted her, "Hello, little girl." A new person came into all of our lives.

When her daughter was two years old, Sarah and her husband went through a rough period in their marriage. Sarah had friends who had left their husbands and she would have had a circle of support but she decided to work it out with her husband because "Our daughter loves her father and needs him." I understood this on the one hand as a powerful devotion to her child and on the other Sarah's wish to change the course of her own history of a missing birth father. Sarah also knew first hand about loving her father Harry who raised her.

Sarah and her husband appear to have worked things out well. They have a meaningful life together with warm friends and family, and he is a devoted father and husband.

Both Matthew and Sarah included Harry and me in their searches from the start. When a parent has to relinquish a child for adoption, it is of course in its very essence a painful story. It takes enormous courage for an adopted child to reach out into the unknown having no knowledge of who or what they will find. It also requires the capacity to be more curious than fearful. Fortunately, all the people Matthew and Sarah encountered in their searches were remarkably sensitive and warmly responsive. I am reminded of Anne Frank's writing in the midst of the atrocities of the Holocaust, "Despite everything, I believe that people are good at heart".[4]

And to take all this into the next generation, Matthew and his wife did not conceive, and they now have two adopted children, a son, and a daughter.

Our family is saturated with the mystery of provenance. Where do we come from? Who are our parents? Who are we? Matthew is strikingly tall, fair, long-limbed and northern European. Harry and I are relatively short Ashkenazi Jews. People who don't know us wonder where we got such a tall son. Sarah is blond with brown eyes. She is also of northern European heritage, but like Harry and me she is relatively short. I am dark, and Harry is fair, and so they see her coloring as a combination of ours. When people do learn that Sarah and Matthew are adopted they invariably ask if they are biologically brother and sister. They put the same question to Matthew's son and daughter.

Who are you? Who am I? We are so hungry to know who begat whom and how we are linked to each other.

Matthew and I went out to dinner the evening after our visit to Post Street. For the first time, he asked many questions about John. He wanted to know about his theatrical career, what plays he was in and about his wives. On hearing about John's decision to become a cadaver, he wondered if John's move to San Francisco was for him "...the end of the line, the outermost edge of the country, maybe a suicidal wish. Jumping off the Golden Gate Bridge is a spectacle, a theatrical way to die."

The next morning we took a long walk through many of the beautiful neighborhoods of San Francisco, in such contrast to The Tenderloin.

---

4   Frank, A. The Dairy of a Young Girl. Eleanor Roosevelt(Introduction) and B.M.Mooyaart (translation). Bantam, 1993. ISBN 0-553-29698-1 (paperback). (Original 1952 translation)

Now in this bright place, Matthew spoke more about what he knew about his birth father, which is very little. He didn't know if he might pursue a search. Matthew also spoke about his children's adoption and we together wondered if they might ever want more information about the circumstances of their birth.

Like Harry, Matthew is a devoted father, husband, and son. They both show up and stay for the long haul. Three men, Harry, Matthew, and Sarah's husband now break the chain of vanishing fathers. For me, abiding men have made all the difference.

Matthew's presence in San Francisco was balm. His willingness to bear witness to the darkness of John's life and to the place where John lived and died helped to wake me from the dream-like state I felt during my first visit to Post Street and saw my reflection in the photograph of John's building. Imagining John was always dream-like. Matthew's questions and willingness to join the journey made it feel real. After he left to return to his family I thought, "John's disappearance did not destroy me. I have a scar for remembrance that I can feel, so real I can almost touch, but I have no open wound."

Just before my flight home I walked alone to 1082 Post Street once more. Discovering the place of John's death now felt moored to earth. The streets were real. I could feel the pavement underfoot, the gravitational pull of walking uphill, the sounds and smell of fumes from passing cars and trucks. I could look into the liquor and convenience stores, the motorcycle repair shop, see the sign on the Diva club saying "Karaoke Tonight" and again look into the Lush Lounge. I thought of going into the Lush Lounge but somehow couldn't. I can't account for it. Was it too invasive? I don't know. Entering the Lush Lounge and looking around felt too much like being an investigative reporter. At that moment I was the daughter of a father who died. If in fact I was not John's biological daughter, at that moment I adopted him as my father. I was trying on what it feels like to be the daughter of a father who died. A daughter arranging a funeral, a daughter burying her father's body, putting a shovel full of earth on the grave, arranging for a gravestone. The stone would say. "John Grandin Pote, born too soon to have a life as his true self." In 2015 when the Supreme Court passed the same-sex marriage act, I burst into tears hearing the news. My first thought was, today John might have had a better life, and I might have been able to know him.

Now as I write this, I feel identified with John in a new way. He was a writer; although by selling the first acts of his plays he thwarted his chances of finding satisfaction in his talents. Through my life long curiosity about him, he is so much a part of me that now I feel he guides me to write. I feel his presence in a new way. Having adopted him, I hope I have taken in the best of him.

When I arrived in San Francisco in 2008, it was 38 years since John's death. He was nowhere to be found in San Francisco. What I found there is how powerfully he exists within me. I don't know if I was ever in his thoughts. The relentless presence of John Pote's absence will not capture him. But it will capture the John Pote I create from this quest. Maybe he would be pleased with the play on the words pot and Pote. He was a word-gamer, and so am I. The shards are his. The pot will be mine.

1959: The First Shard

"You must be in love, or you would not have tried to find me."

I imagine when a pot is reconstructed the archeologist keeps returning to the original shard to build on its lines, its curve, its color. Without the original shard, no pot with a history of the old can be reconstructed.

Fall of my senior year in college, 1959, I turned twenty-one. Harry and I were in love and planning to marry in June. My mother told me, she had learned some years earlier, that John had moved from the City to Westchester County and lived there with his mother. My college, Sarah Lawrence was near his town. Did she tell me in response to my asking her where he was or did she volunteer the information? I don't remember. It could be either. She may have eliminated him from my life, but she certainly kept him in her thoughts. I considered contacting him many times during those four college years but put it off. I was reluctant to open that mysterious box, fearful of what I would find. Was he a crazy drunk who would demand I take care of him? Was he a decent man who hoped that someday he might hear from his daughter? I was leaving the area at the end of the school year. I thought I must try to find him now. It was not only unfinished business but also neglect of an unknown part of myself. Also, I struggled with the question of whether I was capable of loving a man. I had no memory of living with a man I loved, not even a brother or a close cousin. Could I really love Harry if I never loved my father? Is what I felt for Harry real or was I just relieved to find a man who loved me?

I wrestled with whether to let my mother know I was going to contact John. I decided to tell her. Was I trying to be fair or hoping she would tell me not to, or was I contacting him for her? Soon I would be leaving home permanently. Did she or I want them to have a reunion? She didn't stop me. She was single then, although involved with a married man whom she realized was not going to leave his wife. She spoke about ending that relationship.

I called John's number. A man answered the phone. "Is this John Pote?" I asked. "It is." He said. "This is your daughter, Joan Pote." There was a pause. I imagine he was catching his breath. "I'm a senior at Sarah Lawrence College, near where you live. Would you be willing to meet me?" "Yes, I would. Should I come to the college?" The thought of him coming to where I lived made me panicky so I quickly countered with, "How about meeting at that restaurant near the Bronxville train station." "Oh, I know the place." He said. "That would be fine."

He was amazingly poised given my call coming out of nowhere. I could have written a letter first. I had found his name in the phone book. I knew his address. In fact, before I called, I walked by his house—a modest frame house in a working-class neighborhood. I could see there were ceramic figurines on the windowsills. But I didn't write a letter. I think I wanted to shock him, to strike, to take him by surprise—not give him the chance to either think about it or ignore it. I wanted his first response, which could have been "No" or "You have the wrong John Pote." or, "I have been hoping for this call now that you are twenty-one years old." Was he poised because my mother had already called and told him I might contact him?

On the phone, what struck me first was his voice. He spoke in a voice similar to William Buckley, the former editor of the National Review. It is a speech affectation sometimes heard in New Yorkers who think of themselves as upper class or heard in actors who want to sound British. After our awkward greeting at the doorway of the restaurant, we sat in a booth. I studied his face seeing nothing of myself. He was fair complexioned with light hazel eyes. I could see the remnants of a handsome man but he was somewhat bloated and ruddy. His hair, once auburn, was flecked with gray and receding. He wore wire-rim glasses. He must have noticed me looking closely at him and in an apologetic voice said, "I have grown so portly." He was around fifty years old.

I asked "Do you have other children?" he answered in his exaggerated, melodramatic voice, "You are my only issue."

He said his mother, who he had lived with, died a few years before and after her death, he married again, this time to a woman much older than himself. He added she was devoutly Catholic. She liked to collect figurines of saints. Silently I thought to myself, "Those were the figurines I saw on the windowsills when I secretly walked by his (or her) house."

I asked about his career. "I traveled in Europe and the States for a while performing with a repertory company. Now I occasionally ghostwrite political speeches for local politicians."

I told him I had been a dancer before college. I thought about returning to it but was seriously considering that I did not want the life that most dancers led. He asked, "Why not?" I think I said things like little time for personal life and the end of a career soon after age forty. He seemed bored. I suspect my response came across as bland and beside the point. Now I think if I could have given my real answer at that moment it would have been, "I am afraid if I become a performer like you, I could end up like you."

As we spoke, he drank heavily, ordering and re-ordering glasses of beer. He soon became tearful and maudlin saying, "Your mother was the only woman I ever loved." As we left the restaurant and as I waited for a cab to go back to the college, he slipped his arm through mine. It felt like too much, too close, too quickly. I immediately wondered if he was confusing me with my mother. I think he was and I felt sickened by it. I didn't want to see him again. But also in the course of that meeting, perhaps before he drank too much, he said, "You must be in love or you would not have tried to find me." I had not said anything about Harry or being engaged. Now I wish I had had the foresight at that moment to ask what he meant.

I was shaken and confused by the meeting and immediately made an appointment to see the college psychiatrist. After telling him some background and about the meeting with my father he said to me, "You can tell him you don't want to see him again." I felt relieved but over time I came to wish he had instead said something like, "You may decide not to see your father again or you may be able to work something out with him but you don't have to make that decision right away." Then I imagine him adding, "Come in to see me for a while and we can talk about it so you have some time to think about it." I don't remember if I told the psychiatrist that my father said, "You must be in love or you would not have tried to find me." I feel sure I did not say that I thought in his drunken state he may have confused me with my mother.

My father soon called and asked to meet again. I think I said something like "No, It's too difficult for me." With the same poise I heard in our first phone call he accepted it, and we never met or spoke again.

At first, I felt relieved, but over the years I grew to regret I could not manage it better. I told my mother I met with John and decided not to see him again. I don't think I said more than that, perhaps only that he drank heavily during our meeting.

For a long time, I did not fully take in his words, "You must be in love, or you would not have tried to find me." They remained only words, but words I couldn't forget and stood out separately from the rest of the meeting. I may have first thought it was a conceited or self-important remark to make. Slowly another possible meaning emerged. When I first saw how our daughter Sarah, even as a young toddler was so loving toward Harry and attached to him, I had to ask, "Did I love my father when I was a very small child?" I wanted his words about needing to find him to mean he recognized that at some early time I loved him. Now I was in love and bringing my first love of a father to someone new. If I could hold onto that meaning of his words, I could also believe that inside John Pote, in spite of his artifice and neglect lived a person who could be thoughtful and had some real substance. I hope it is true. What he said came to feel like a late received gift and the first solid piece I had of him. It helped me to trust that I really loved Harry. I wasn't merely relieved to have someone love me.

Could it be that John once loved me? I can never know. I most want to believe I once loved John and that he knew it. As important as it is to feel loved, and it is crucial, it not as crucial as believing I can love someone else. Loving another is how I know I'm not an empty vessel.

Good Morning

When I returned from San Francisco in 2008, I found I was preoccupied with why John decided to move there. Was it "the end of the line" as Matthew had suggested or was he looking for, hoping for, a place where he could safely be himself and live his sexuality, perhaps find someone to love. From what I learned about his illnesses and death I imagine him to be a suffering man seeking either relief or release from his life. It is highly unlikely I'll ever learn the facts. Fiction will have to do.

Out of breath, John struggles to walk up the Post Street Hill. It is an August weekday, mid-morning in The Tenderloin district of San Francisco. The year is 1964. John, a man in his fifties, is on his way to the Lush Lounge on the corner of Post and Polk. But the hill is steep, and John's gait is unsteady. His hands shake. His old brown pants are too long, so the cuffs gather over his shoes. A short-sleeved shirt of some yellowish synthetic fabric strains over his swollen belly. He wears wire-rim half-glasses. They lend his once handsome face, now puffy and flushed, a remnant of dignity.

He enters the bar timidly, holding back the door as it slowly and quietly closes. He wants no one to notice him. Gingerly he pulls himself onto a barstool at one end of the bar and orders a beer and a shot. Swallowing the shot in one gulp, he sighs then hunkers down over the beer.

The bar is old, smelling of stale, beer-saturated wood. The upholstery on the bar stools is frayed. Above the bar is a large photograph of the Golden Gate Bridge. In the window, under a Four Roses Bourbon advertisement is a bouquet of dusty artificial roses.

At the other end of the bar sits a woman with an empty cocktail glass in front of her. She is in her mid-forties wearing a pale blue taffeta cocktail dress. Her make-up is heavy, her lipstick dark and a little smudgy. She has big blond hair and wears shimmery costume jewelry. A long pink chiffon scarf is wrapped several times around her neck. She calls to the bartender, "Hey Bill, another Manhattan here." Her voice is hoarse and gravelly.

"You've had enough Berta. It's time for you to go home. It's 10:30 in the morning. You were here when we closed up at 2:00 AM. Where've you been since then?"

"It's none of your business Bill."

You've had enough Berta, you need to go home."

"Don't tell me what to do Bill. I'm fine. Just make my drink."

Bill makes the Manhattan, gives it to her then turns his back to set up for the day.

Berta takes a large swallow. She lights a cigarette and stares at the smoke as it lingers in the air. She suddenly notices John and studies him. John stares into his beer glass. Clearing her throat, Berta asks "You new here, mister? I haven't seen you before." In a monotone, not looking up, John mutters "yeah".

The bartender, busy setting up the bottles, appears to ignore them but is also listening. Every once in a while he looks over his shoulder. Berta won't be put off. "Oh yeah, just moved here? Do you have a place?"

Visibly annoyed, John wants to be left alone but maybe not. "I just moved down the street." then sharply, "OK?" Berta winces at his sharp tone. Then comes back, "Yeah, yeah—that's fine. Where you from?" John drains his glass and motions to Bill for another. Bill draws the beer and John takes another swallow before answering her. "New York." Berta is encouraged, "New York, wow! I've never been. Why would you come to this God forsaken place? Some people call it the end of the line." She points to the picture of the Golden Gate Bridge. "We had another jumper last week. It happens all the time here. I've known a lot of people who jumped. One survived. He was a cripple for life. He hit part of the bridge on his way down, landed on his back and then was on his back for the rest of his life. He finally died of lung cancer. I think he must have been glad to go finally. But yeah we have a lot of jumpers here. They take this life for as long as they can, and then they jump." John, turning his back on her, muttering sarcastically "Thanks, I'll take it under careful consideration." Again Berta persists. She is hungry to talk even if John is not listening. "This part of the city is a dump—no one ends up here because they want to be here. No one starts drinking here in the morning if they have somewhere else to go. I'm here 'cause I hate my apartment. My mom is there. She's in a wheelchair. Her legs were cut off after she got diabetes. She still drinks. She stinks. And she's crazy. I hate going back there. That's why I am here. She takes a swallow of her Manhattan, then another. "You're a good-looking guy. What's your name, handsome?" Reluctant and obviously uncomfortable John mumbles, "John" and turns further away. "So John," She takes her drink and unsteadily saunters closer to him, then around him so that he is forced to face her. She moves in close. John recoils. She startles and backs off. "Oh! Oh! I'm sorry John. I don't mean nothin." She moves to a bar stool still facing him but at a conversational distance. "I just want someone to talk to, John, that's all I want. I can't go home yet. Can you talk to me John? Can you do that for me John? Please, please." She starts whimpering then crying pathetically. She takes a crumpled tissue from her purse and dabs at her wet mascara. "Please John, just talk to me. I just need someone to talk to me. " Taking a big gulp of his beer John sighs. He reluctantly pulls her toward him. She wraps her arms around his neck letting her weight fall against him. Feeling her body close, John starts to cry—big convulsive sobs. His head is now on her shoulder and he is crying into her neck, into the chiffon scarf. As John sobs, Berta regains some composure. "It's ok, Johnny. You have yourself a good cry. You aren't thinking of jumping are you? We've too much of that here. Johnny—you're a nice looking man. I bet you've had some pretty gals interested in you. I bet you can find a nice lady friend who will help you out—get you back on your feet—give you a few laughs." She gives a forced laugh then implores, "Maybe I can be that nice lady friend Johnny? Maybe huh? But maybe you have a wife at home. Do you, Johnny?" John, still sobbing, "She kicked me out."

"Why'd she do that Johnny—sure you drink—is that the reason? I had a guy kick me out too but I'm better off without him. He'd kick me in the shins yelling—'Just a little shindig dearie—You like shindigs don't you?' Why'd your wife kick you out, Johnny—nice looking guy like you?" John sobs intensely. Berta orders him another shot. He gulps it down. She takes a cigarette from her purse and lighting it from her own slips it between John's lips. He inhales deeply and is more composed. He now looks directly at Berta and for the first time speaks directly to her, "I'm sick. I can't help it. My wife caught me wearing her bras and panties. I started when I was eight. I'd sneak into my mother's dresser and put her underwear on. Later I was supposed to go into the army and my mother, the bitch, wrote them saying I was a homo and not to take me. I didn't even know she knew what I did. I was able to keep it a secret from my wife for years. But then she caught me all dressed in her stuff, and she kicked me out. She was disgusted by it. She kept calling me a crazy pervert. She kicked me out."

"Where'd you go Johnny?"

"I stayed with my mother for a while but that was Hell. I had to get far away."

"Johnny—you came to the right place. Do you know The Diva Club down the street—it's for men who like to dress up. You can have some fun there and not feel crazy. The people are friendly."

"I know about The Diva. Someone at McSorley's talked about it."

"What's McSorley's"

"It's a men's bar in New York. Not quite like The Diva Club. That's why I came here. What I've done I've only done in secret. For me, it was always my secret. I don't know if I can be out."

"I want to help you, Johnny."

"How can you help me? Why do you want to help me? "

"I like you, Johnny. I can talk to you. I can tell you are a good person." Unwinding the chiffon scarf from her neck, "Here Johnny here's my scarf." She wraps it around his neck and puts her rhinestone clip-on earrings onto his ears. She takes off his glasses and puts them into her purse. She pulls back and stares at his face. Then from her purse, she takes out her lipstick, her eyebrow pencil and her mascara setting them down on the bar. Tenderly she applies the lipstick showing him how to hold his mouth like hers as she applies the color. She delicately fills in his eyebrows with her eyebrow pencil raising her own brows as she does it. She carefully holds his eyelids open while lightly brushing the mascara onto his lashes. She pulls back to look at her work. "You look good, Johnny." John moves his face feeling the applied cosmetics. "Here, see how good you look." She takes out a compact and opens it. He looks into the powdery mirror and nods. "I'm going to walk you over to Diva's Johnny. They know me there. I'll go in with you. You'll be with friends.

We'll have some fun". John tentatively puts his hand on Berta's cheek. "My god—YOU"RE a guy! You have stubble."

"Don't worry Johnny—everyone is a friend here. I want to help you. Come into the men's room for a minute." They squeeze into the small men's room.

"Give me your pants and shirt and your socks and shoes too." Berta slips out of her dress and high heels. They dress in each other's clothes "And take this too, Johnny." She takes off the blond wig and puts it on him.

"Why are you doing this for me? I don't even know your name and you don't know me."

"I'm Berta, Johnny."

"Berta?"

She looks embarrassed. Hesitantly she says. "Well I was Robert— Now I am Berta."

"Berta—Why are you doing this? What do you want from me?

"All I ask of you, Johnny, is that you talk to me. Please, please talk to me Johnny. That's all I ask." They leave together, John hobbles in Berta's high heels but Berta holds him firmly by the arm. The door closes. The bartender watches them walk toward Divas. He lifts his own glass in a toast, his lips forming the words "Good morning".

PART II

EMPTY PLACES / EMPTY SPACES

How does empty space shape us?
We imagine, we dream, we create and if we are lucky,
we find what we yearn for in new editions.

Cast of Characters

<u>Father</u> (missing) John Pote (I called him "Daddy" or "John")

<u>Mother</u> Marion Friedman changed her name to Marion Glenn, married John Pote, Irv Kahn and Caleb Stewart (I called her "Mommy" and later "Marion")

<u>Maternal Grandmother</u> Fannie Seigel married to Marvin Friedman, changed her name first to Stephanie and later Frances Glenn (I called her "Mama")

<u>Maternal Aunt</u> Anna Friedman changed her name to Natalia Glenn or Natalia Garcia (I called her "Natalia")

<u>Maternal Uncle</u> Leonard Friedman (I called him "Lenny")

<u>Maternal Grandfather</u> (missing) Marvin Freidman

<u>Maternal Great grandfather</u> (missing) Marek Selzer

<u>Maternal Great Grandmother</u> Malkah Selzer

<u>Husband</u> Harry

<u>Son</u> Matthew

<u>Daughter</u> Sarah

Empty Places/ Empty Spaces

For three generations fathers went missing. This memoir is the story of how members of each generation tried to shape and sometimes fill our empty father spaces. We remembered or invented. We imagined or convinced ourselves we didn't need the missing person. Sometimes, like the husbands and fathers, we too abandoned one another. Sometimes we pretended the missing father was not really missing, believing he would return. Or we said, "He's dead".

When my grandmother was fourteen, her father left her mother in Poland with eight children. Soon my grandmother was sent first to Budapest and later to America to work and send money home. Then another sister joined her. The family, who remained in Europe, all perished in the Holocaust.

When my mother was ten, her father left her mother with three children. When I was two, my mother left my father and soon my father disappeared from my life. Each missing father ultimately severed all ties with his children.

At various times four single women, my mother, her sister, my grandmother and I lived together in a New York apartment. We called our household the "girls' dormitory". My mother's brother lived elsewhere with his wife and remained with her but they had no children. My aunt never married nor had children. My father was an only child and had no other children that I know of. With no siblings or cousins, I became a generation of one.

While each of us coped with our empty father spaces in different ways, one shared way amongst the women of the family was to change our last name, our father's name. We also changed our given names as well.

My grandmother was Fannie Seigel, a Jewish immigrant from Poland who married a Jewish Hungarian immigrant, Marvin Friedman They had one son; Leonard called Lenny and two daughters, Anna my aunt and Marion, the youngest, my mother. Anna was the most flamboyant of name changers. She changed her name to Natalia. Anna/Natalia also changed her last name from Friedman to Glenn. At one point, when she lived for a time in Florida, Natalia pretended she was Cuban and Catholic and changed her last name to Garcia, but when she moved back to New York, she again called herself Natalia Glenn. Leonard, simply called "Lenny" did not change his name. He remained Leonard Friedman, but he mocked the women for altering their names. Lenny would call Anna/ Natalia only NAG, initials for "Natalia Anna Glenn/ Garcia." My mother, Marion went along with the last name Glenn until she married my father and then took his last name. She married three times and always took her husband's name as her last name. She briefly changed her first name to Jackie but soon returned to Marion. My grandmother also went along with Glenn, erasing her husband's name and changed her first name from Fannie to Stephanie because she thought it sounded less Jewish. But ultimately she settled on Frances Glenn.

Leonard, Anna, and Marion all called my grandmother "Mama" and so did I. Outsiders assumed "Mama" was also my mother and that my mother was my sister.

I did not escape my own identity alteration. My mother, who preferred I call her "Marion" rather than "Mommy," which I eventually agreed to do when I reached young teenage, told me when I was born they had not chosen a name for me. Why? Why couldn't two people, immersed in theatre and Shakespeare choose a name for their coming baby? I would love to have the name "Miranda", or "Olivia" or "Viola" or "Katherine".

At times my mother felt compelled to tell me stories most mothers might censure, or at least wait for their children to grow up. I was around thirteen or fourteen when she told me John wanted her to have an abortion and later in her pregnancy wanted her to put me up for adoption at birth. My mother said she was unwilling to do so. She added that when I was born they both wanted to postpone giving me a name, claiming it would give me the opportunity to choose my own name. Choosing your own name is like buying your own birthday present. I also wondered whether not choosing a name was still leaving adoption an open possibility—as though there was an option to try it and if you don't like it, return it.

Apparently, the hospital would not discharge mother and baby until the parents chose a name and wrote it on the form. So they hurriedly wrote Joan Marion, Joan for John and Marion for my mother. Naming a baby for the living in Jewish tradition is heresy. I suspect my mother knew that but ignored it.

Apparently sometime after my first birthday, John and Marion began to call me "Toni." In the 1930s the word toney or tony was a term meaning trendy or classy. My parents spelled it Toni as they might spell the nickname for Antonia, another name I would have been glad to have. However, I do think of their coming up with "Toni" was some indication of happier feelings about my existence. Maybe it meant that adoption was now off the table. "Toni" stuck but when I grew up, left my profession as a dancer and later established myself in the realities of the regular working world; I had to account for my non-name, not quite a nickname. "Toni" sounds so different from "Joan".

By the 1970's I often wondered if my now normal looking life, being married, having children and meaningful work was real or if I was playing a part I wanted. I wanted to feel real and the first thing I did was to retrieve my real legal first name, Joan.

I don't like the name, Joan. It has a closed and gloomy sound like drone or moan. However, Joan is my true name. It was given first. It is the feminine of my father's name and so it is another way I hold his place and his space in mind. In dark moods, I feel I was never given a name. Anyone who knows me from before my thirties still calls me Toni. If they meet me recently and know me mostly in the presence of my husband who calls me Toni they usually switch to Toni quickly even if I have initially introduced my self as Joan.

I can only imagine the stormy beginning of John and Marion's life together. Marion says John already was drinking heavily. Life probably grew more turbulent when a baby landed in the scene. When I was around twelve, Marion told me John proposed to her on her birthday by handing her his newly minted, gift-wrapped, divorce papers. Then Marion and John secretly ran off and eloped. According to the story, they went missing for days. Marion further embellished the story, telling me that while on the run to find a Justice of the Peace willing to marry them, they slept in the same bed and "John was such a gentleman, he did not touch me until after we married." What was I supposed to make of this tale? Was Marion telling me not to have sex until I was married? Was she telling me that John was so confused about his sexuality that he panicked when she was in bed with him? Was Marion suspecting, but trying not to know about John's bi-sexuality? The story goes on. Mama, frantic about her daughter's sudden disappearance, did not seek help from the police or friends but instead, she and Natalia frantically ran from one New York library to the next thinking "Marion likes to read. Maybe she is in the library." (This is all so bizarre. Did I really hear this story or did I imagine it?) Finally, Marion showed up, and Mama and Natalia had no choice but to accept that Marion had eloped with John who they, especially Mama, hated because he was "a wild, drunken, waster."

So I learned that Marion and John, both paupers and John an alcoholic, moved into a one-room basement apartment on Charles Street in the Village. I suspect that when Marion became pregnant, the thought of adding a baby to the situation was absolutely overwhelming. I can only imagine they put the pregnancy out of their minds, went on with their bohemian life, their parties, their heavy drinking and John regularly disappearing into McSorley's for a night on the town. I imagine they could not, dare not, let themselves think about their future with a baby. The inevitable happened, and I was suddenly in the scene.

1940: New York—Who is Who?

Later I learned that in 1940 when I was 2 years old, my mother left John and moved uptown to my grandmother and Natalia's apartment the "girl's dormitory" located on New York's upper-west-side.

My mother needed to find a job to support us. At that time it was difficult for women with children to find work. Employers preferred to hire unmarried women with no dependents. Worried about this, my mother wanted me to pretend she and I were sisters and I should call her "Marion". She thought it would be an easy transition because we both called my grandmother "Mama". Apparently, I refused to go along with it and insistently called her "Mommy."

After a crash course in typing and shorthand as well as lying about her marital and parental status she found full-time work as a secretary in an advertising agency. Over time she had a variety of different jobs in different settings.

Mama was my primary caretaker when I was between the ages of four and ten. We were always together. Sometimes Natalia or my mother lived elsewhere. There were many moves, and I changed schools frequently.

Then in 1948, my mother re-married, and I moved in with the new couple. That marriage lasted less than two years. After, my mother and I lived alone together until I left home for college.

Natalia was an artist who worked for department stores creating window displays. She never married and was secretive about her romantic life. She had two long relationships with women. First, there was Pat, and later there was Jess. Over time Natalia lived with each woman for a while but never declared these couplings as romantic. Ultimately she left each woman, finally returning to live with Mama until Mama died in 1978. After 1978, as far as I know, Natalia lived alone.

Lenny was a traveling salesman married to Gloria. They lived in Brooklyn and had no children. He kept his last name Friedman and never denied he was Jewish. He scoffed at the women's name changes as "phony". While his manner was contemptuous, I also found his stance offered some solid ground to stand on. Perhaps Lenny's way to dismiss his father was never to become a father himself. He took on no fatherly role with either his sisters or me. He and Natalia, if they ever spoke of their father at all, referred to him as "the old man." My mother, however, called their father "Papa."

Once my mother landed her job, the question remained who was available to take care of me. After several unsuccessful efforts to cobble together a plan, I was sent to one of the few existing all-day children's nursery schools. Usually, Mama brought me to and from school. I soon learned that others were confused because I called her "Mama." They assumed she was my mother. I remember a conversation with my teacher when I was around four that went something like the following:

I am chatting on with her about Natalia. My teacher looks puzzled and says, "Who is Natalia?"
"She is my aunt."

"Is she your Mama's sister?"

"No Mama is her mommy."

I thought Mama is your mommy

"No, Mama is my grandmother."

"And who is the lady who says her name is Marion? Is she your sister?"

"No. She is my Mommy."

"What do you call her?"

"Mommy."

"What does "Mommy" call your grandmother?"

"Mama"

"And you call your grandmother "Mama"?

"Yes."

"What does Natalia call your Grandmother?"

"Mama"

"So you all call your Grandmother "Mama"?

"Yes"

"Do they all take care of you?"

"Yes."

"Aren't you a lucky girl you have three mothers!"

I doubt I was able to address this at the time, but if I could have, I would have said, "No, I have one Mommy, one Mama, and one Natalia." I wish I also said, "I have one Daddy who I sometimes visit." This was during a time when there were still occasional visits with John.

The conversation in nursery school was an early example of sorting out who was who. The comment about "three mothers" was repeated many times not only by people outside of the family but also by Natalia and Mama; less so by Marion. I suspect that seeing other children with their fathers' led me to ask why John did not live with us. I remember

44

Mama saying with seriousness, "You have three mothers so why do you need a father?" After all, we were three generations without fathers. We were surviving well enough. Weren't we? With time I heard, "Why do you need a father?" as a real question, "Why do I need a father?"

Over the next twelve-years, the girls dormitory went through many re-configurations. There was a steady stream of departures, returns and changing apartments as well as the entrances and exits of new characters in the lives of my mother and Natalia.

I insisted on calling my mother Mommy through young childhood but by the time I was a young teen, it seemed babyish. I tried to call her "Mom", what most of my friends called their mother's. But she claimed she didn't like it and again proposed I call her "Marion". I still resisted and she accepted "Mother" which I tried for a while and then could not stand the formality of it—so I gave in and agreed to call her "Marion". By then I began to have a life outside the family and could hold in mind she was indeed my mother whatever I called her. At least Marion started to with an Mmmm sound.

Stories

Mama, my mother, and Natalia were all talkers who sometimes told their stories—or at least parts of them. I often asked each of them to tell me about their childhoods and also about my early life. I loved to hear the stories, even the sad ones about how poor they were when their father left. Stories with their beginnings, middles and endings helped to make the constant changes of day-to-day life somehow less confusing. What happened now could be told later. These stories sometimes revealed how they dealt with their missing fathers.

My mother was a particularly dramatic storyteller. One of her favorites took place soon after her father left the family.

"There was a fire in the apartment building in the middle of the night. We were all in bed when the fireman banged down the door and grabbed me out of bed. I guess he grabbed me because I was the smallest. This burly fireman stood at the top of the stairs and threw me down the stairs to another big fellow at the bottom who caught me in his arms. Then Mama and the two older kids ran down and out of the building."

What a great story—the fire, the danger, being grabbed out of bed by a stranger then thrown down the stairs and caught in the arms of another big strong stranger. What must have been terrifying turned into a thrilling game of catch between two rugged men with their powerful, protecting arms, just when my mother's father had abandoned them all.

I think my mother lived out this story for the rest of her life. She longed for and was excited by men. She never gave up wanting a man, and like the scene with the fire she went from one to another but curiously and sadly every man she chose and every man she married, and she married three times, let her down.

1942: The Green Grass School

Before my fourth birthday the all-day nursery I attended in an Episcopal Church closed for the summer. My mother and Natalia both worked full time and Mama, either didn't volunteer or wasn't asked if she could step in and so I was sent to spend these months in an orphanage. It was located somewhere on an estate in upstate New York and run by Episcopal nuns. I don't know the name of it but because of the huge grassy lawns surrounding it I called it "The Green Grass School". I think it was my not quite four-year-old effort to make my place of exile into something more appealing. Wasn't it good for children to get out of the city into the country? Possibly that is what I was told.

My mother left and there I was with about a dozen boys and girls I didn't know. We slept in a large, bright, white room in white metal cribs lined along each wall. The Green Grass School became my measure of despair for all future painful situations of utter loneliness and fright.

I was heart-broken, desolate and hopeless. I tried not to feel alive. It was too painful. I didn't want to eat, gagged on their food and was constipated. Most mornings the nuns gave up waiting for me to have a bowel movement and finally sent me out to play with the other more productive and compliant children. I lived in suspended animation waiting for my mother to come and take me home. It was as though I would not agree to live for anyone, but her and I would resume living only when she arrived. If I could have held my breath for the duration, I would have. I held back what I could, allowing little to go in and little to come out.

On alternate nights the nuns bathed us in large washtubs, each of us lifted in for a quick efficient wash then lifted out. Another nun toweled us dry. We children were treated with indifferent kindness. We were all exactly the same. We were jobs to be done. I remember screaming, "I don't want a bath now. My mother will give me a bath when I go home." Calm efficiency ruled the day. The nuns did not get ruffled or angry. They proceeded with their tasks wordlessly—lifting, washing, toweling, dressing and putting to bed. Once we were all in our cribs with the metal sides noisily lifted into place, and the lights turned off, the room filled with sobs until the last of us, exhausted, surrendered to sleep.

There was a farm on the estate. On the evenings without baths, we visited the cows, goats, chickens, and pigs. I found some comfort in visiting the animals. Maybe because they ate greedily, eliminated freely and played joyfully. Visiting the farm animals were the few moments of the summer ordeal when I didn't feel my body under siege. Or perhaps they reminded me of visits to the Bronx Zoo with my mother. There I would be lifted into the young children's petting pen to play with the rabbits and lambs.

If my mother visited Green Grass during that summer, I don't remember it. Maybe she did visit but her leaving again was so painful I can't bear to remember it. Finally, thankfully, at the end of the August, she arrived, and I returned to live in the "the girls dormitory".

Long after returning from exile, I might have been about six, my mother and I again went to the Bronx Zoo and then the zoo took on a darker aspect.

I wanted to go on an elephant ride. The parents stood on one side of the elephant path while the children waited in line on the opposite side of the path. But when that enormous elephant came lumbering down, I was scared and ran to my mother crossing in front of the approaching mammoth. My mother leaped over the fence and pulled me to her while we backed against the fence letting the beast pass.

But why did I run in front of that oncoming hulk? Was it only that it looked monstrously big and I wanted to get back to my mother quickly? Was it more than getting her to rescue me? Did being at the zoo and near animals again bring back The Green Grass School with all its misery? Is it too far fetched to wonder if I was declaring the world as I knew it and feared it, to be too much—better to be dead? I don't know. But I do know I have always needed an ace in the hole in case life was too difficult or disappointing. The plan could be as benign as thinking, "I can always disappear by reading." At times it has grown into a detailed suicidal plan. Making a plan suffices as my escape hatch — no need to act on it.

The Green Grass School to this day remains my measure of misery. If it is not as bad as that, then it is bearable. Looking back, I suspect the isolation and loneliness were the worst part of it.

On my return when my grandmother, Mama, saw my skinny, miserable state, she was appalled. She told me later that I looked like a war orphan. She knew only too well her fear and loneliness when she was sent away from home at too young an age. She never saw her mother again.

Her difficult early life continued well into her adulthood. But by the time she was fifty, her three children were finally all adults. Lenny, her son and Natalia, her eldest daughter financially supported her. At that point in her life, she could have enjoyed some freedom. But she renounced it to do what for her was the right thing. At age fifty-four, Mama stepped-up and took on my care full-time. I suspect she saw it as an act of decency and duty. And maybe she saw in me her sadness at being sent away. From then on, until I was ten and my mother re-married, Mama and I were always together. She called us "the two musketeers." But I wanted my mother, not her and I suspect Mama wanted her freedom, not me. But I was not as despondent as I was when I was sent away. Nothing could ever be as bad as that Green Grass summer.

The baths given by the nuns may have become such a focus of my grief and fury because they were in such contrast to my mother bathing me.

After she came home from work, always the high point of my day, she lifted me into the tub, often with bubbles added. She soaped me with her hands then lifted me out, wrapped me in a big towel while I cuddled into her lap and grew warm again. Then she put on my nightgown, combed my hair and told me I was a "glamour girl."

But often she was not home. Then Mama bathed me. It was far more perfunctory and efficient than my mother's way although not as quick and matter-of-fact as the nuns. However, it also was like the nuns because when Mama bathed me I missed my mother intensely. In anger, I shouted at her, "You're a bad boy!" Mama angrily called the rambunctious boys in the neighborhood "bad boys" if they did not pause in their game of stickball against the stone stoops to let her pass. Her reaction to my outburst was to call me a "bad boy" back, rather curious in my naked state. Then I returned the volley with a ferocious, "You, you-you, you!" I don't know how she kept from laughing. I laugh now as I remember this. But I believe at those times she and I missed my mother for different reasons. We were burdened with each other—both of us gloomy and very angry.

Later, looking at a photograph of myself before I was sent away and seeing a smiling, chubby-faced toddler, I'd speak to the picture saying, "You look happy now, but just wait. You won't be happy for long. Just wait until you are sent to The Green Grass School. You won't be smiling then." The painful constipation, my sadness, my fear that my mother would never arrive never wholly disappeared but remained a gauge of what was truly terrible.

Still today I occasionally dream that I am living in a huge warehouse, empty except for beds lined along the walls. I am frightened. There are people present but everyone is a stranger. Ware/house—where am I?

Mama, her Children, and her Life

We were three generations, but we functioned as two—Mama and her children. Lenny, Natalia and my mother were the adult children able to be on their own, and I was the young one at home with Mama and still in her care. By then I no longer had any contact with my father.

Lenny was married and living elsewhere and except for his time in the army and after he retired stayed in one place. But the females in the family were constantly on the move. Natalia and my mother sometimes left Mama and me alone together, often for months at a time, while they each pursued new jobs or new romances. Also, Mama and I together did our share of moving, first back and forth to Florida where Lenny was stationed in the Army and then back again to New York. I changed schools so often they became a series of isolated islands. Friends were brief encounters. My world was in constant motion. I always missed my mother but Mama was a steady presence.

I suspect it was difficult for her to be my caretaker. She had already done it for her younger siblings and her children with no help. She could be withdrawn and depressed. It could be lonely for both of us. Her bitter experiences had become part of who she was. She could be harsh, possessive and even tyrannical. But she showed up predictably while the others didn't. Because of her I never went to another Green Grass School and probably avoided foster homes and boarding schools as well.

Later I met two of my mother's friends, Georgia and Liz, both working women and like my mother both divorced. As far as I knew they lived alone. Each had one child, but I never met those children because they never lived with their mothers. They were in boarding schools and during vacations they lived with relatives. I always lived with Mama.

Mama's life seemed relentlessly severe. Except for her son Lenny, she wanted nothing to do with any man. When her children were ages fourteen, twelve and ten, Marvin, her husband, deserted the family never to be heard from again. There was never a legal divorce. Mama hated Marvin even before he left her. The story goes that Mama found him in bed with her best friend, Becky. Apparently, Mama felt terrible and was embarrassed for Becky because Becky had been subjected to Marvin's "disgusting advances." I suspect Mama renounced sex if she ever embraced it. As far as I know, she never had anything to do with sex or romantic love after Marvin left. She was only in her early thirties.

When I was a young teenager, I once asked Marion (by then I was calling her Marion instead of Mommy) about Christmas and the Virgin birth. She told me that Mama had a theory that Mary's father impregnated her. Marion thought that was a plausible explanation. This puzzled me at the time but the memory of hearing this lingers. Why? Does it speak to something that happened—happened to Mama or her sisters—is that why fathers disappeared? Did something happen to Natalia and Marion with Marvin? Is it a fantasy? I don't know and never will, but Mama's hatred of Marvin and John and her renunciation of men and sex at still a young age leaves me wondering.

More than once I heard Mama say, "As long as you have a mother you don't need a father except for what he earns." Also, "Who needs it?" or "You don't need that!" were refrains, not only about men, about most things that were not essential to survival. As long as you have enough food, clean clothes and a roof you don't need more. You renounce what is missing. You relinquish wanting.

Mama (originally Fannie) was the fourth of eight children, five girls, and three boys. She was born around 1888, into a German-speaking enclave in a Polish town. Her exact age was unknown because there was no record of her birth. Her language with her family at home was Yiddish. At school, she spoke German and in the town spoke Polish. Petite and fair with cat-like green eyes she attended school until grade eight then left school when her father left the family to move alone to the mountains. The reasons given for his exit were vague and multiple. "He got sick with tuberculosis." He was badly beaten in a pogrom". Whatever the cause he never returned.

At first, Fannie stayed at home to help care for the younger children while her mother and older siblings supported the family. They worked for a company that managed a salt mine. Then around 1903, Fannie was sent away, first to Budapest where she worked in a relatives grocery store and later to New York's lower east side. Her relatives in New York soon arranged a marriage for her with Marvin, a recent immigrant from Hungary. Fannie would have been about nineteen. She became pregnant quickly but had a miscarriage. Then within a year, she gave birth to their first child Leonard or Lenny. Two years later Anna (Natalia) was born. And two years after that Marion, my mother arrives.

There is an old faded photo of the three children when they were about eight, six and four. Lenny, curly-haired sits straight up in his chair. He is smiling and in command. Anna/Natalia, tall for her age with the strikingly straight black hair, high cheekbones, and dark eyes, inherited from her Hungarian father, stares starkly into the camera. Marion is petite and softly pretty. Her head tilts as she smiles coyly. Perhaps her father takes the picture. Marion is the only one who ever spoke warmly about Marvin. She believed she was his favorite, that he preferred her, his younger, more delicate and pretty daughter. Marion recalls him criticizing and scolding the older two but not her. She told some of her happy memories of him. He loved music. Every Sunday morning she woke to opera on the Victrola and the smell of corn muffins baking in the kitchen. Lenny and Natalia had only harsh words for Marvin. Marvin, after more sexual dalliances and a gambling habit, deserted the family. They did not hear from him again. If there were ever photographs of him they were destroyed. Marion described him to me as tall and thin with jet-black hair and high cheekbones. She considered him handsome. After he left, Mama went to work in a hospital kitchen and soon Lenny and Natalia took jobs as well. Lenny worked as a delivery boy and Natalia sold candy in a five and ten cent store.

I remember Mama as often stern and tight-lipped. She quickly became furious, especially toward my mother and me, lashing out and slapping or she took to her bed feeling ill or exhausted. I know now that during this period, the early 1940's, her family in Europe stopped writing to her. Later she concluded the Nazis must have rounded them up and they disappeared into the torments and ovens of the Holocaust.

Mama had a younger sister Rivka, who married a man from Vienna. They immigrated to New York in 1940. Mama and Rivka refused to speak Yiddish together even though it was their first language. Rivka changed her name to Rima, and she and Mama spoke only in German or English. Eavesdropping on their conversations I first heard the name Hitler and the word "Schweinhundt," both spat out like curses.

Mama's lonely immigration, her miserable marriage, her husband's desertion and the disappearance of her family in Europe left her and

Rivka/Rima the sole survivors of their family of ten. Then in the late 1940s Rima left for Palestine/Israel where she soon died of leukemia. Mama was now her original family's only survivor.

Mama was fifty when I was born, and only fifty-four when she took over my care. By then she must have had enough of children and their demanding needs. But the pattern was familiar. For two generations she took care of fatherless children and so she would take care of me as well. I suspect her already thwarted life again felt curtailed. Like other loses and deprivations she may have again told herself she didn't need or even want more than she had. But she did need and want control over her daughters. She waged many bitter arguments against their "wild" behavior. Natalia was secretive about her life. Marion was more outwardly rebellious. Because Mama was stuck with me she could readily accuse Marion of "neglect" or call either of us, "you ingrate".

Mama always made sure I had the right food, warm clothes in winter, shoes that fit, a hat to protect me from the summer sun. She was efficient and matter of fact in her care but unlike the nuns at The Green Grass School she was prone to fits of rage. After these, she often complained of "feeling weak" needed "to lie down." She lay perfectly still on her back with closed eyes. Sometimes I checked to see if she was breathing.

Or she could shift into intense action. Watching her do housework I could read her angry body bending over the bathtub scrubbing the clothes on a washboard then lugging them to the roof to dry—all the while scowling, scowling, scowling. If the day was sunny, summer or winter, she lugged the rugs up the stairs of the apartment building to the roof. I had to go with her because she was afraid to leave me alone in the apartment. "There could be a gas leak or a fire! Gypsies could break into the apartment and kidnap you!" With me climbing the stairs behind her, carrying the wicker rug beater, she hauled the rugs onto the apartment roof that always smelled of tar. Then she heaved them over the clothesline and furiously beat them. I sat on the little divider that separated our five-story building from the attached next building. I watched her angry face and listened to her rhythmic grunts as she beat out the clouds of dust from each rug. On other days she might walk all over the city paying the gas or electric bill going directly to the company and handing over the cash. She must have been physically strong to do all that she did in the way that she did it, but she thought of herself as having frail health.

When Mama took over my care her physical anxieties did not stop at the borders of her body but extended to mine. If I leaned out the window to watch a screeching fire engine, she was sure I'd plummet to the street below. Then holding her heart she'd whimper, "I'm going to faint! Quick—the smelling salts!" She kept them in her purse.

I was not allowed to play with children in the neighborhood because they had colds or were rough. She feared I'd get hurt or catch an illness or die on her watch. My slightest sniffle or even a rainy day was her cue to keep me home from school. I missed many weeks of school. I loved school and felt cheated. But there was a reward. On these at-home days she showed me a different side of herself. She was more relaxed and at her best. She made appealing snacks of tea with cookies from a local bakery. We listened to all the radio soap operas. She told me stories about her sisters and brothers and also about her parents who were first cousins. They all lived in the foothills of the Carpathian Mountains. She told me about rolling down the hilly terrain and climbing trees, the family cow and their few chickens. On our days of truancy, instead of her daily trips to the A&P Super Market with me in tow to help carry the bundles home and up the stairs to the apartment, she phoned the upscale Gristede's Grocery Store and had them deliver food for the day. She might order a chicken and show me how she removed the pinfeathers. Then performing an autopsy, she pointed out the various organs including the insides of the gizzard that might contain a few small stones and some kernels of corn. Then she threaded a needle to sew up the eviscerated chicken securing the legs and the wings. In these moments I felt close to her, and I believe she looked to me as her companion, her fellow "musketeer". But I was always relieved and happy to get outside and back to school.

When my mother and Natalia lived with us, they worked days. Nights, they were often out and on the town. Natalia, an artist, was part of the bohemian art scene of the thirties and forties. My mother wanted to enjoy her dating life, especially at the Stage Door Canteen where she volunteered as a hostess and then dated some of the men. Both Natalia and my mother earned additional income working as life models at the Art Students League.

Mama and my mother had terrible screaming arguments. One morning Mama started shouting at my mother while she was still asleep after a night out. Mama accused her of "traipsing around" and "neglecting" her child. My mother, of course, woke suddenly to Mama's barrage. Distraught and furious my mother screamed back. I don't remember what she screamed, but Mama coldly turned her back. Then my mother in rage ripped off her pajama top so that all the buttons came popping off leaving her bare breasts exposed. I was shocked to see my mother so out of control, her face so contorted in rage, saliva spurting from her mouth as she screamed back at Mama and so vulnerable with her bare breasts. Days of Mama's cold silence and my mother's tears followed. Frozen with fear and sadness, I tried with no success to comfort my mother. After a while life went on as usual—until the next tirade.

Freedom Run—A Trail Toward the Future

In spite of my mother's "traipsing", until I was a teenager, I was deeply attached to her. I barely saw her during the week, except briefly at the end of the day. But on weekends she devoted Saturday and Sunday daytime to me and brought me into the world. She recognized how confined I was all week in the apartment with Mama. We went to all the New York museums, the Zoos, children's theatre, Isadora Duncan interpretive dance classes held at some Communist organization and to the Automat for lunch. And then, as part of these adventurous days, we went to the Sheep Meadow in Central Park, and there she shouted out "Run!" She knew I needed space, movement, and speed. I ran until she was almost out of my sight and then ran back to her and into her arms. It always felt so good, and I always wanted to do it again and again. Then I zigzagged across the field, then ran backward, then spun around and around until I was dizzy. I loved the risk of falling and not knowing where I was heading.

It was about leaving and return, leaving and return and about freedom and taking risks, taking charge of my body. I was drunk on the pleasure of it. I felt the desire and urgency to run away and equal urgency to return. I felt relief from being confined and the joy of doing what I wanted to do.

The ecstatic childhood pleasure of Sheep Meadow was the seed that grew into the passionate freedom I came to know first as a dancer and later as a psychoanalyst.

Dance and Psychoanalysis

As a dancer, I loved to jump and leap, defying gravity. I loved to surrender to lifts while still sustaining form, strength, and rhythm. I loved daring to trust the lifter who in those days was always a man. I loved daring to trust that the other dancers would also keep the beat—otherwise we could collide or they might not show up where they were supposed to be. And dance movement uses the skill of the body to express feeling

Later, those freedom runs in the Sheep Meadow and dance transformed into the freedom I experienced during psychoanalysis— freedom to think, feel and say all I wanted to in the safety of trusting the psychoanalyst and the psychoanalytic discipline. With the psychoanalyst I learned to attend to the shifting movement of my thoughts and feelings as I left the linear paths of narrative to zigzag toward and away from digressions, fly backward to memory then forward to the present, associating all to current feelings and situations. If thoughts are like scenes or landscapes, feelings are like the climate of those landscapes. Sometimes feelings evoke thoughts and other times thoughts evoke feelings.

The frame of the fifty-minute hour, the set time and place, the constancy of the psychoanalyst holds reality in place while the patient's mind flies to where it will and then reflects on the journey.

The dancer and the psychoanalyst both train for many years to strive for freedom and honesty. The body, in gesture and expression, reveals the nature of the person. The body can be trained to move in complex ways, but no two people and no two trained dancers move precisely alike. Each dancer, particularly if they will become a soloist, seeks suppleness, power, and their own idiom. The psychoanalyst and patient seek the personal truth behind clichés, illusions, assumptions and distorted beliefs.

Dance and psychoanalysis merge visually in this drawing that hung on the wall at the end of the psychoanalytic couch in my office. It was created and given to me by a colleague Dr. Eric Taswell. It is very spare. From four curving sweeps of a calligraphy brush emerge the powerful opposing stretch and sweep of the limbs, the buoyant breath filled torso and the ecstatic arc of the neck and head all conveying passion, freedom and the thrilling defiance of gravity tempered by a controlled return to earth. When I saw the drawing for the first time, it looked at first like a Japanese icon. Then out of the curves and the white spaces, I gasped as I saw a human figure leap into view as she descends from a grand jeté.

Some patients while looking at the image used the figure to embody their own experience. Some saw the limbs powerful opposition as paralyzing conflict, freezing the figure in space. Others saw the controlled descent as the loss of illusion. Some looked at the figure's skillful flight and trim body enviously. At moments of retreat and caution some disembodied the figure and spoke about the lines, "Two are parallel but then they veer off from each other". Almost everyone who spoke about the drawing returned to it later with new perceptions. Most at some point saw the dynamic thrust of the dancer's leap as freedom regarding it wistfully, hopefully, desirously. For me, this leaping figure is a metaphor capturing the essence of an ideal analytic interpretation— laconic, dynamic, deeply felt and down to earth.

The drawing of the leaping dancer was of course fully in my view as well as the patient's view. We both could choose to see it or not. The drawing reminds me that there is no mind without the body and the body leads the mind. All feeling begins as a bodily feeling. Pain, cold, heat, hunger, satisfaction, comfort, the impulse to cry or laugh or moan starts in the body. The mind finds ways to convey what the body feels through gesture, expression, voice tone and ultimately language. Sometimes people ignore emotional communications from their body and try to be only rational and intellectual. And sometimes people shut out their emotional pain by focusing only on their physical aches and pains—wittily know as an organ recital. Language is full of visceral allusions to emotional experience. "It hit me smack in the gut." "She's a pain in the neck." Or more spicily, "He is an ass hole." or "She pisses me off."

The drawing was a constant reminder to me to listen to both body and mind. Patients make themselves known not only by what they say but also by their posture, muscle tension, stomach gurgles, shifts in the tone of their voice.

Also, as an analyst, I sat behind the patient and out of view. This allowed me to be more physically relaxed so I too was freer to tune into my visceral responses to patients such as becoming tearful or restless or sleepy.

Recognition of how those freedom runs in the Sheep Meadow led to dance and how dance led to psychoanalysis was a winding and slow route. The connections were not evident for many years. A different experience led to the actual decision itself to begin the arduous, lengthy and expensive process of psychoanalytic training.

This is the Grand Canyon. But which Grand Canyon is this?

It was 1985. I was in my mid-forties. Our children were teenagers, preoccupied with friendships, the beginning of their love lives and future work interests. I was a clinical social worker, working in clinics and private practice as a psychotherapist. My work was mostly satisfying, but as I continued to study and participate in clinical conferences, I came to know several psychoanalysts. It was soon apparent that their understanding of their patients and how our minds work was far more in-depth and fuller than mine. They were mostly psychiatrists who at the time were the only ones accepted by The American Psychoanalytic Association, the largest American psychoanalytic organization that set standards for clinical training. My local psychoanalytic institute was a part of The American Psychoanalytic Association and therefore shared their standards. This was very different from the European and South American training models that already had a long history of training non-medical psychotherapists in psychoanalysis. There were a limited number of American non-medical mental health professional psychoanalysts who were accepted for training but only as researchers, not clinicians. I was a non-medical clinician, not a researcher and therefore ineligible.

Then in the mid-1980s a group of psychologists brought a suit against The American Psychoanalytic Association for restriction of trade and won. As a result, clinical training in psychoanalysis by institutes belonging to The American Psychoanalytic Association opened for non-medical mental health professionals. The training at my local institute consisted of a personal psychoanalysis, which took as long as was needed for the individual and therefore varied in length. A five-year curriculum of classes, as well as supervised clinical work, was required. The training was also expensive and time-consuming. It could easily take between five and ten years. Did I want to commit myself to such an undertaking? I could not decide. I had other interests, including writing and music. Where was I going to focus my time and energy as our children became more independent and left home to pursue their own lives?

Around this time our family made a trip to the Grand Canyon, and we journeyed part of the way down. We returned home, and I became obsessed with the idea that I needed to return and get to the bottom of it. So on Labor Day 1986, I went back to the Grand Canyon, this time without my family. I needed to climb down that last funnel of black schist, to stand on the banks of the vital, roaring Colorado River. However, never really being an out-of-doors person, I felt terrified of going into the wilderness. I would be at the mercy of surprises of all sorts, weather, poisonous animals, falling, dehydration and getting lost. I took the cowards way out and chose to ride down on a mule with a group. As I climbed onto the saddle, I had the sensation of climbing onto the broad shoulders of a man. Suddenly I imagined myself enthroned on John's shoulders, and riding tall. Had I ever ridden on John's shoulders? I don't know, but the sensation was unmistakable.

I immediately bonded with my mule, a lovely, large, black animal named Sox, in honor of his white leggings. Sox somehow convinced me he was not bent on suicide and would not suddenly jump off the trail into the rocky abyss below. Before starting down the Canyon, the mule driver came by to check my saddle and asked where I was from. Immediately I said "New York" and startled myself. I had not lived in New York for more than twenty years. This was already more than a journey into the Arizona wilderness; this was a journey into memory.

The Grand Canyon is a marvel of the natural world, with switch-back trails, slippery scree, arid deserts, subtropical forests, precipitous drops, soaring heights, darkness, brilliance, wildlife, suddenly appearing side canyons and always another place beyond the last place visited. The amazing massive scale of the Canyon cannot be captured on the widest of movie screens. The relentless play of light on the Canyon walls grants dynamism to solid basalt, granite, and schist. These rocks carry the story of geological time, but not in neat linear layers. Like old memories, old rock rises to the surface because of shifts in the earth. Wind, weather or water pushes old layers to the surface, so that old rock becomes a part of the more recent rock.

Hawks and longhorn sheep suddenly appear and disappear like curious creatures then quickly return to their busy invisible lives. The roaring, muddy Colorado River ceaselessly creates the Canyon to be deeper and deeper. There is no getting to the final bottom of it. As long as there is a river, there will always be more. This seemed to parallel the thought that as long as we live, there will always be more to understand. The descent to the bottom of the Canyon was thrilling, but though I became wet with the waters of the Colorado, a full sense of getting to the bottom of it eluded me. What was I looking for?

As I rode back up to the top of the canyon, thoughts about pursuing psychoanalysis rose up again. The vastness, intricacies, and challenges of the Grand Canyon was a metaphor for the vastness, intricacies and challenges of our inner-world, perhaps the grandest of canyons with its own switch-back paths of memory, thoughts, feelings, dreams, fantasies, body sensations, desires, and fears.

I made the decision. First I would begin a personal psychoanalysis and then consider the possibility of training.

I planned to meet with several analysts and decide who felt like a good fit. It only took one meeting with the first analyst.

Explaining my reasons for seeking psychoanalysis I told him that life seemed to be going well. Harry's and my relationship had weathered some hard times and now felt sturdy. Our children were on a good course. But how could this be true for me? Was my life real? It was now so different from what it had been as a child. Was I only pretending to be different from three generations of fatherless and unmarried women? Was my life just made of wishes and illusions? Would I lose everything I thought I had? Then blithely, I commented, almost as an afterthought, "I have no siblings or cousins." His response was, "That is a lonely position." Suddenly I had a lump in my throat and I knew he had slipped under the radar, not to what I didn't already know, but to what I tried not to feel.

I began the personal psychoanalysis in 1988.

On the night before psychoanalysis began for the first session, I dreamt I was descending the Grand Canyon on foot and there was a brass railing to hold onto that would offer support all the way to the bottom. I suspect this stood for what I hoped for from the psychoanalyst. The brass railing also reminded me of a brass footrest in an old fashioned bar and grill located on the corner of the apartment building where we lived with Mama. When I was small and occasionally visited that bar and grill with my mother or Natalia I was almost as close to that railing as an adult would be to a handrail. As a child, I often wondered if John might be in that bar. Memories are landscapes and landmarks.

After a year in psychoanalysis, I decided to pursue the training

To be in psychoanalytic training is to be in psychoanalysis four or five times a week, to see at least three control patients four to five times a week, to be in supervision and in classes. At some point, this happens all at the same time.

It was exhilarating to attend the classes, to do the reading and to listen to patients who had committed themselves to this intense and time-consuming effort to understand their lives. At times it was painful to confront myself in psychoanalysis, to feel sadness and pain I had put aside. But it was also gratifying to see old confusions through a fresh, less distorted lens.

With the help of a trustworthy guide, the process of bringing past feelings out of the past and associating them to present experience where they can be looked at from the advantage of no longer being a helpless child is what makes both the past and present feel real.

I also experienced some of the same pain and exhilaration while training to be a dancer. Training to be a dancer at the very least gave me a new sense of control of my body and taught me discipline. Analytic training teaches patience and the power of listening to other people and to one's self. As I journeyed through both my psychoanalysis as well as classes, control cases and supervision I needed new metaphors to explain the experience. I needed even more than the spatial, visual and sensual metaphors of the Grand Canyon. Music and drama served this well.

I continually listened to Beethoven's late quartets. This music represents pain, reflection, joy, and ecstasy as well as the breadth and humanity that is part of listening to patients and becoming a psychoanalyst.

The Cavatina, which is a part of quartet 130, is an exquisitely tender private meditation full of passion, yearning, and sorrow. Towards the end the music begins to steadily pulse first gently and then gets stronger as it moves along. It is like waking from a long preoccupying reverie and tentatively, carefully re-approaching the world. The movement that then follows is a loud and rhythmic dance with the instruments all actively engaged and playing off one another. The dramatic shift from having turned deeply inward to re-joining the world of others is close to what it feels like to emerge from a powerful analytic session and then to plunge into the hurly-burly of the outer social world.

Dennis Potter's splendid B.B.C. television script, "The Singing Detective," was the right drama at the right time. It is about a man, a middle age writer with crippling psoriatic arthritis who searches his memories, dreams and his imagination for the meanings of his current physical and emotional pain. Among other things, he confronts the profound loneliness of his childhood.

When I was ready to end an eight-year psychoanalysis, I was confident enough to trust my stream of thoughts and to experience them independently of someone standing by. I owned my thoughts and feelings with all their shifting contradictions and tangents. I felt free to speak them or choose not to speak them. I had learned to tune to the dynamism of my patients' minds as they struggled with desire and constraint and wrestled with what they didn't know about themselves but would come to know, perhaps with pleasure, sometimes with chagrin. I was most gratified by the work when they grew interested and familiar with observing the movement of their own minds; watching their thoughts sometimes put on the brakes and other times more freely move through memories, dreams, imaginings, emotions and body sensations, catching familiar recurring themes, "There I go again!" or "Here I go again!"

Now, many years later after enjoying the deep satisfaction of a career in psychoanalysis, there is a certain painful pleasure to know I will never get to the bottom of it. Our inner world has to be at least as vast as outer space. And like space, there is no clear, up or down, only more. But only more means that as long as there is life and the life of the mind, the journey continues. And paradoxically, the more I learn about the inner world, the actual world becomes more real.

The 1940s: Running From and Running Toward

On our mother-daughter Saturday outings together my mother always dressed beautifully often in treasures she unearthed at Klein's Discount store on 14th street where samples or clothes worn by fashion models were discarded for sale at drastically reduced prices. She also sewed for herself and for me, making me dresses with embroidered designs. To me, she glowed with beauty and the excitement of the world. I lived for my weekend times with her.

She enjoyed my adoration. She often said, "You are my greatest audience." I had to grow up before I recognized how much she needed that admiration and how much I needed to give it to her. I doubt she gained much satisfaction from her work as a secretary. She enjoyed her good looks and dressing well. She enjoyed being pursued by men. She liked to say, "I am chased until I am caught" It took me a while to get it.

She had women friends but often lost touch with them, made new friends and lost touch with them as well. I think, in a big sisterly way, when she wasn't in the frantic pursuit of a man, she enjoyed me until I reached late teenage and our relationship began to have more conflicts, especially over my developing separate life and romantic relationships.

But as a child, my precious time with her was refreshing and exciting. Her life seemed glamorous, so different from Mama's drab, stay-at-home, constricted, housedress life, fueled by fear that whatever war and pestilence caused all her relatives in Europe to disappear would soon arrive in New York and eliminate her and her American family as well.

Beginning when I was five years old Mama, and I spent even more time alone together. Every year my mother and Natalia sent us away for months at a time. Our destination for these, usually three-month long deportations, was Miami Beach, Florida. I left school in New York and went to school in Miami Beach for a few months. The girl's dormitory all agreed that going to the South would protect my delicate upper respiratory system from colds and croup. I don't know what I thought then, but now I don't believe that was the reason. I had the usual childhood colds and croup but recovered from all of them. What I do believe is that the three women needed long vacations from each other. It was their version of "Freedom Run."

Why at that time did they choose Miami? Why in spite of Mama's fears of illness and death was she willing to go to a hot climate where the polio epidemic, then rampant during summers in New York, was even more virulent throughout the year in Miami? Everyone knew someone with polio who was either paralyzed or dead. I suspect Mama wanted a respite from her "wild" daughters and Marion and Natalia certainly wanted to be free of their domineering mother. But even more compelling may have been the fact that Mama's only son, Lenny, her oldest and favorite was in the army stationed in Miami Beach. He was a drill sergeant. His job was to put his charges through exhausting exercises in the hot sun. For his efforts, the recruits humiliated him with merciless anti-Semitic epithets like "you dirty kike." Mama was no stranger to , and I suspect this explained her urgency to be near Lenny. The first time Mama and I went Florida I left Kindergarten in New York around October, and we stayed in Miami Beach for the winter months, There, Mama offered solace and home cooking to Lenny. We lived in a small apartment on Miami Beach where Lenny often visited.

I thought about my mother constantly and probably daily asked when I would see her again. Even when my mother was living with us if she said she was going out that evening my stomach dropped as a sob rose in my throat. There would be nothing to look forward to at the end of that day except perhaps a radio program, maybe Jack Benny, Truth or Consequences or Mr. Keen, Tracer of Lost Persons. They might get me through. And when I tried to settle to sleep at night, I curled up into a tiny ball telling myself I was curled into my mother's lap. But when her absence stretched into months I sometimes could not remember her face. I couldn't picture it. Panic gripped me.

Telephone calls were expensive and rare. There would be some precious letters from her, perhaps one a week. She might describe going to a nightclub or out for a pancake breakfast or a Sunday bike ride through Central Park with a man she was seeing or a trip to the Museum of Modern Art. My hunch about the three women needing a break from each other rather than their proffered claim that I needed a warm climate was confirmed when two years later the deportation was reversed. Mama and I stayed in New York for the full school year of my second grade while my mother left to work and live in Miami and Natalia went to live with a woman in Palm Beach Florida.

Living alone with Mama was like living in a sealed, sterile bubble. At moments it was cozy, but the rest of the world was locked out. Curiosity about the world and the people in it was dangerous at best and at times utterly toxic. If someone was not related by blood, they were called "strangers." She did have two "friends" who she rarely saw. One was Becky, the woman she found in bed with Marvin. Becky visited once every year or so. Another, Mira, was a loyal neighbor at the time

Marvin left the family. Mira lived out of town, and her visits were also rare. Eventually, contact with both ended.

I suspect when Mama first left her home in Poland she probably was at the mercy of strangers. Her childhood world disappeared into the cinders of Europe. Her husband vanished. Along with her need for respite from her daughters she also feared some horror would befall them when they were out of her sight.

The three adult women of the girls dormitory all needed to run and tried to, but as far as I can tell none ever felt free. I am forever thankful for those freedom runs through Sheep Meadow. I know and in various ways have always known that they became the iconic vision, the pointer and the guide for life decisions. It was an experience of being both thrillingly untethered and still deeply connected. That brief activity with my mother nearby on weekend afternoons powerfully helped me to imagine and shape a life. Being both free and connected became my compass for choosing work and who to love.

The Third Mother

My aunt, Natalia Glenn, sometimes Natalia Garcia, mother number three, was named Anna Friedman at birth. Of Mama's three children, Natalia most revealed her Hungarian father's Magyar heritage. Her sculptured facial structure, dark eyes and raven-black hair gave her an intense and exotic appearance. She was twelve when her father deserted the family. As an artist, working in window display, Natalia yearned to be a part of the Bohemian art scene of the 1940s. She found friends who were part of it, but Natalia herself was never a recognized artist. Early in her twenties, she stopped dating men. She darted in and out of our lives, sometimes living with Marion, Mama and me and sometimes living with her women partners. She had two ongoing relationships with women, Pat and then Jess, each lasting four or five years. While we all knew them both, Natalia never clarified that they were romantic partners and I don't think anyone ever asked if they were.

Natalia, although headstrong and secretive, was also brutally self-critical. She believed she had failed as an artist and I suspect also struggled with being a Lesbian

While Mama was critical of my mother's flamboyant sexuality, she was accepting of Natalia's secrecy and her rejection of men. However, she complained bitterly about both daughters spending so much time away from home.

Unlike my mother who capitalized on her delicacy and femininity, Natalia was lean, muscular and strong and usually dressed in paint-spattered work-pants and men's work shirts. It was only after Natalia died, and I found among her things a love letter to her from Jess, that I could more surely guess that Natalia did, in fact, live her life as a Lesbian. I imagine that Natalia, like John, struggled painfully and secretly with her sexuality.

Although my mother was the little sister, she always gave Natalia a hard time. Relentlessly bossy, she continually criticized Natalia, especially her clothes and her friends. Natalia never gave it back to her, never told her "Cut it out!" or "It's none of your business!" but instead listened looking contrite and ashamed. As far as I know, she never revealed her secret life to a family member. My guess is that my mother sensed Natalia's sexual preference for women and it made her nervous.

As I grew older my mother criticized me for not being girlish or feminine enough. When I was a young teenager she regularly clipped out a column from a woman's magazine called, "How to be a girl" which I always tore up unread. My mother was preoccupied with who among her single women friends might be a Lesbian. Once, during a heavy snowstorm when she was out for the evening with a woman friend, Gayle, they decided to stay overnight in a hotel rather than risk no public transportation during a blizzard. I was about twelve at the time. For reasons I will never understand she needed to tell me the next day that she thought Gayle might be a Lesbian and proposition her but she did not.

Did my mother fear I might turn out like Natalia? In fact, I look more like Natalia than her. Natalia and I share some traits such as the need to move. She was a fidget, and so am I. Although she was not constant at all in her presence, she was constant in expressing her love for me. Many times I have had the fantasy that Natalia, after an experiment with a man, became pregnant with me. I also can imagine she gave me to my mother because my mother was married at the time. I doubt this is true, but it recurs as a fantasy.

Everything about Natalia was urgent and intense. She read and re-read Proust, all seven volumes of the Scott Moncrieff translation. She read all of them over and over. I suspect she found comfort in Proust's struggle and exploration of sexuality, especially between same-sex couples.

She liked to think of herself as part Gypsy or Latina. Choosing her name, Natalia, and her Cuban-Garcia period was an aspect of this. She lived and worked in Florida for a while and during that time affected a Cuban accent that she maintained every day. The strain and need to do that must have been exhausting. When she returned to New York, she again assumed her Natalia Glenn identity free of the Garcia and accent but still of Latina heritage. She never missed the opportunity to walk in the annual New York Puerto Rican Day Parade.

When I was a child, and she was present she was always ready to play games with me—but she was too much all the time—she was a wild playmate and sometimes scary. She liked to put Gypsy or Latin music

75

on the Victrola, pick me up and ferociously dance like a dervish around the apartment until I felt terrified that the sheer force of her movement would send me flying. If we were outside, she might suddenly say, "let's run!" One time, I was about eight, we were on Third Avenue, and as the elevated train roared overhead, she grabbed my hand and ran so fast my feet left the ground. It was so different from the bucolic freedom runs in the Sheep meadow where I was in charge of my body. When I tried to run with Natalia, she was utterly in control, and I was overpowered.

If I had a project for school that had an element of art in it, such as making a diorama that portrayed a moment in history, she provided all sorts of good paper and paints to complete the project, which I appreciated. Yet she could get so into it that she sometimes took over. I vividly remember "Cortez in the Hall of Montezuma". She offered to paint a marble floor for the castle. She did, and it was perfect, but I worried the teacher would criticize it as obviously not my work.

When I started to dance, Natalia also started to take dance classes at the Martha Graham Studio. Perhaps I was her second chance of childhood—but she was always too much.

Natalia evoked a lot of fantasies for me. She was the tallest of the women in the family as well as the strongest. I knew she was a woman, but I thought of her as the man of the family, curiously, more so than I thought of Lenny as the man of the family. If there was lifting or heavy work to be done Natalia rushed to do it.

I probably cast Natalia in the missing place of my father. Maybe Natalia cast herself in the missing place of her father.

When I was around four, I fell and put my tooth through my lower lip. It bled profusely. Natalia picked me up, and with my mother walking beside her she carried me to a local doctor's residence and office. It was night. I was lying across her arms and in spite of all the blood and pain, it was the first time I remember seeing the night sky filled with stars. I must have asked, "What's that?" Because I remember or imagine, Natalia saying, "Those are the twinkling stars. They shine in the night. They are always there even in daylight. But we can see them only when the sky is dark." Their light was dazzling. This event of pain, fright, affection, excitement and magical beauty captures life with Natalia.

I once spoke to Natalia about my wish to fly. We had a long discussion about how many balloons it might take to accomplish lift. We also considered a trampoline and a pogo stick.

Natalia was imaginative, witty, loud, clever and a madwoman. There was no place of calm within her. One rare time when I was alone with her she wanted to broil lamb chops. They soon caught fire and the apartment filled with smoke. She managed to put it out but it was all part of Natalia. If Natalia cooked, of course, there would be a fire.

My mother was very different from both Mama and Natalia. She could be madcap, like Lucille Ball or Gracie Allen. If some syncopated tune came onto the radio, she might break into a goofy dance. Her soft, prettiness was like some of the movie stars of the day, Claudette Colbert or Jean Simmons. Her flirtatiousness drew people to her; both men and women found her charming. As problematic as my mother was for me I knew she was not crazy. When she was good, she could be very good. She also could be very selfish, angry, bossy and very sad but not crazy.

Natalia was a dervish. People found her interesting, exotic, unique, and infuriating. Natalia and Mama unlike my mother were rarely madcap. They could be mad-crazy. All three could be mad-furious.

As soon as I reached my teens, Natalia often made admiring comments about my body. It made me excruciatingly uncomfortable. I became very self-conscious and cautious to not in any way provoke her interest. She could also be extremely provocative with strangers. She enraged bus and cab drivers by angrily and shrilly criticizing their driving. Age did not subdue her. In her sixties, she and I walked past a

Greenwich Village jazz club. At the door stood a hugely muscular man, the club's bouncer. Natalia impulsively went up to him saying, "You have a beautiful body." The man looked surprised but kept his poise. I asked Natalia why she did that, and she said, "As an artist, I appreciate beautiful bodies."

When Natalia ended her last relationship, she came home to live with Mama, and utterly devoted, even enslaved herself to her tiny, possessive, domineering mother. By then Mama was in her seventies. The sign on their apartment mailbox read, "Natalia and Frances Glenn." If someone overlooked the feminine spelling of Frances, they might think a married couple lived there.

Their lives together, which lasted almost fifteen years, became for me a vision of a mother/daughter nightmare. The two of them soon became entwined in a Gordian knot of desperate clinging, resentful fury and the terror of losing one another. Could I end up like that with my mother?

Mama became more confused and fearful during the last five years of her life. Although still physically strong, she claimed she felt weak if she left the house. If Natalia went out and was late returning, Mama greeted her with either frantic crying or rage, at times even impulsive violence. Mama might hit her or pull her hair. Fearing it was unsafe to leave Mama alone, Natalia soon was housebound as well. "She could fall, she could start a fire at the stove."

I raised the possibility of bringing in help or perhaps a nursing home. Natalia was adamant that she would never leave Mama with strangers or send her to a nursing home. "I won't throw my mother away!" is how she put it. Who was the prisoner and who the jailer?

While writing about this, I dreamt Natalia called saying, "You have to help me. We all must live together again!" I awoke startled, thinking, "No, no, no!" Then I was reminded that when I traveled to visit my mother after her last husband died, I always had the terrifying fantasy that I would fall ill or be in an accident and trapped alone with her, never again to return home to Harry and the children. My childhood dream of being alone with my mother had become an adult nightmare about all three mothers.

1978: New York—Mama's End

Finally, Mama took things into her control and refused to eat. As she slowly drifted toward death, she called out for her mother, "Mama, Mama." Within a month, she died of pneumonia. She was approximately 89 years old.

The funeral took place at a Jewish funeral home on the Lower East Side, probably within walking distance of the tenement she first lived in when she arrived as an immigrant from Eastern Europe. A Rabbi no one knew conducted a brief service. Did Mama asked for a Rabbi to be present or did Natalia make that decision? The rabbi read from Proverbs 31, the standard text for the death of a woman.

A woman of valor who can find? For her price is far above rubies. The heart of her husband doth safely trust in her, and he hath no lack of gain. She doeth him good and not evil all the days of her life.

The rabbi didn't know Mama's history and so totally missed the poignancy and irony of what he chose to read.

Natalia insisted on an open casket, unusual for a Jewish funeral, and asked that Mama be dressed in her warm coat and hat "…so she would not be cold." My mother, Natalia, a friend of Natalia's, Harry and I were the only people present. Where was Lenny? Marion and Natalia decided not to tell Lenny Mama died or that there was a funeral. Their decision shocked me. They feared he might have a heart attack if they told him. He did have a heart condition, but they seemed to think they could say to him later, and he would be all right with that. I was even more shocked when that turned out to be so. He claimed he did not mind not knowing Mama died, and he did not mind not knowing about the funeral or not being present. Did they all collude in creating empty places and empty spaces? Was Lenny like Mama? Did he believe he did not want what he didn't have?

It was the saddest, bleakest funeral I ever attended. Later, another funeral would be even sadder.

It took many years to understand and feel the crucial importance Mama holds for me. I believe Mama always feared I would die or kidnapped on her watch. I suspect she had school phobia and that is why she kept me at home as often as she could get away with it. To quell her fears she needed to keep me in her sight. If I strayed, for example into another child's apartment without informing her, she angrily hit me. But her demand that I stay in her sight also meant she was in my sight too. Strangely, even with her terrors, her fury and her violence, this turns out to have been astringent help. She stayed when others left. I could count on her to be there in certain very fundamental ways. She may have been the most difficult person of my young childhood, but she was by far the most consistently present. Mama showed up.

Natalia Alone

After Mama died at age eighty-nine, Natalia was in her sixties. She continued to live alone in their apartment. The names "Natalia and Frances Glenn" remained on the mailbox. One curious change, however, was that Natalia did not want me to come to her apartment which I did not understand until much later. Instead, she made trips to Harry's and my house in Connecticut, or we spoke on the phone. Often in these calls, she was full of regret and self-criticism that she never developed her painting and sculpture and she was especially virulent toward herself for leaving so many of her efforts unfinished. I would make some ridiculous comment like, "You and Leonardo left your work unfinished." She would laugh too heartily and tell me how much she loved me and that I was the "light of her life."

She did get out more, walking miles through the city stopping often at MOMA or smaller galleries. She was a devoted radio listener especially to WBAI, a New York station offering political news and opinion from a leftist perspective,

Her capacity to be outrageous never left her, but as she grew older, she became more and more like a rebellious toddler without a speck of judgment.

After September 11, 2001, when she was ninety years old, she and I traveled by plane to visit Marion who had been sick. Amazingly, after we went through security, she pulled a huge pair of sharp scissors and some white paper out of her purse saying she wanted to "cut out snowflakes". The authorities were very kind and offered to put the scissors in her stored luggage that was still at the counter. I don't think she was demented, but any remnants of constraint on her impulses were gone. We then had a stopover in the D.C. airport, and Natalia ran amuck all over the waiting area, ducking under roped off areas. I raced after her and caught her as you might catch a toddler. And if I could have lifted her onto my lap, I would have.

After Mama died, I began to have more contact with Natalia than with Marion. Marion married Caleb her third husband, in 1964. Caleb and Marion moved to a Maryland and Caleb, who was extremely possessive, discouraged Marion from maintaining her old ties with either family or friends. This was the price for the marriage to last. Marion obliged, and it worked.

Natalia was never critical of Marion for folding under Caleb's demands, but she had only critical words for Caleb. She was convinced he had brainwashed Marion.

While it was always difficult to spend more than short amounts of time with Natalia because she was so unpredictable and so intense, she clearly cared deeply for me as well as for Harry, Sarah, and Matthew. Eccentric and chaotic as she was she made some effort to be parental and even grand-parental. Matthew sometimes took her to lunch at an Asian Noodle Shop she enjoyed. She made clown paintings and cat paintings for Sarah. Sarah hung them proudly in her bedroom showing them off as her great aunt's creations.

When I began psychoanalytic training, she volunteered to send me a substantial sum of money each year to help pay for it. She lived like a pauper and looked like a bag lady but claimed she had squirreled money away and giving it to me, she said, "It makes me feel like my life is worth a nickel." Occasionally she expanded on this by decrying her lack of success as an artist and her alliances with "the wrong people." She only went so far as to say that each of the women she lived with, Jess and Pat were both overbearing and demanded her constant loyalty and attention. Maybe Natalia, like Marion, also succumbed to the demands of anyone who might offer the hope of care and love.

Alongside Natalia's secretiveness and ruses, such as pretending to be Cuban, she sometimes engaged in honest, real talk. When asked about her memories of John she compared him to the role Lawrence Olivier played in the movie, "The Entertainer" a defeated, pathetic, music hall entertainer, now on the skids. She told me again about how she and Marion walked in on John in bed with a man. However, Natalia never spoke about her sexual preferences. Was she was more sympathetic toward John than she dared let on? They shared a lot. Both closeted themselves. Both were artists who got in their own way and couldn't develop their talents.

In brief visits and small doses, she could be witty, even delightful. She too, like John and like me, was a word-gamer. She loved puns as well as any peculiarities about language such as homonyms. Some times she sent me humorous sketches of modern dancers and athletes accompanied by funny captions, not unlike what Jules Feiffer did for the Village Voice. However, in almost every conversation at some point, Natalia needed to tell me some, not at all funny, sexual joke where a man acts like a fool. I have no idea where she heard these jokes. Did she make them up? My ignorance about their origin came from my immediate discomfort when she made any sexual allusion. I urgently wanted to change the subject.

She continued to be a fidget and needed to move quickly. She walked through the streets of New York most days and avoided buses and subways whenever she could.

In July 2002 at age ninety-one, Natalia suffered a burst appendix. After her surgery, she was hospitalized for about two weeks and suffered a variety of complications. During this time she was charming, infuriating, enraged, thoughtful, loving, hateful and sometimes entirely out of her mind. Harry, Matthew, Matthew's wife, and Sarah visited her in the hospital. She adored them and was delighted to see all of them and deeply appreciated their visit. Matthew married a Latina woman, and Natalia was thrilled to have a Latina relative, at last.

However, with male doctors at the hospital, Natalia was extremely hostile and combative. One young male doctor who was assigned to care for Natalia was very distressed and told me she would not let him go near her. He had tried to examine her as gently and as respectfully as he could but after, if he so much as walked up to her bedside, she screamed at the top of her lungs and tried to bound out of bed, pulling out her lines. She was medicated with antipsychotic medication and at one point restrained. One doctor asked me if she had ever been raped. I said I didn't know but could understand why he asked.

I kept Marion informed by phone about all that was happening. She made one visit after Natalia's surgery but it was exhausting for her. She had suffered a stroke a few years before and although for the most part recovered, her stamina and endurance were minimal.

Natalia was not recovering or gaining strength. But in her lucid moments, she rose to the occasion and was direct and honest. She declared, "This is the end." She knew she would soon die. She gave me the information I would need to know after her death. She had no will. However, she received a pension from a union connected with the work she had done and listed me as her next of kin. She told me the name of her bank and also a list of neighbors to contact. She had certificates of deposit in her name. Half of them also carried Marion's name, and another half carried my name. During Harry and my last visit, she charmingly counseled us, "It is important to dance every day—even for only five minutes. Tango is good because it is both fast and slow." As I kissed her goodbye on the forehead, she suddenly blurted, "You want to kiss this poisonous person?" These were her last words to me. Both of her last comments about tango and poison linger. They capture who she was to her very end.

The next day I received a call from the doctor attending her saying she had a blood clot in her lung. The doctor had asked Natalia if she wanted some oxygen. She said "yes." I suspect she thought she was only going to have a small nasal tube. However, she was put on a respirator and sedated heavily. The doctor asked my permission to do a blood clot dissolving procedure that could kill her but added she would surely die if he did not do it. I said, "Go ahead." He called me later that day saying she had died during the procedure. I was relieved. I suspect Natalia would have also been relieved. During her hospitalization, I learned she also had kidney problems and cardiac complications. She could not have gone home. She needed full time nursing care. I know she would have refused it. The restrictions would have enraged her. Being tethered to life support machines would have been pure torture. She died on Independence Day, the Fourth of July, 2002.

Harry and I arranged a cremation.

The Apartment

On July 5th I enter Natalia's apartment. For years she refused to allow me to visit her. Now I can see why. I think I am going to faint but I can't because it is so cluttered and so chaotic there is no safe place to fall. The rooms are littered with pieces of broken dining room chairs and small broken tables all lying on their sides like the wounded dead. I imagine she smashed them to the floor in one of her rages. She left the debris. I can only guess it was to punish herself. She probably forced herself to walk over it and look at it every day. There is a pink upholstered chair torn up as though stabbed with scissors or a knife. From under the junk that lies on top of it, white cottony stuffing oozes out. Dust, dirt, and disorder are everywhere. There are hip high stacks of old junk mail and newspapers with corridors in between. The kitchen is full of empty food jars and bottles.

Hundreds of tiny stickers from individual pieces of fruit are plastered all over the kitchen counter. The floor of every room is covered with old New Yorker Magazines so that walking on them is slippery and treacherous. What rug I can see is discolored and torn. Closets brim with more old junk mail and outdated phone directories. I knew she had a passion for dollar stores. There are dozens and dozens of plastic plates and bowls piled everywhere. Inside the closet hang about twenty pairs of men's khaki pants. Her clothes, many in tatters, are strewn about everywhere. The dust is choking. I must get some masks.

Her bed! Her bed hangs backward towards the floor at a sharp angle, suspended on two front but only one back leg. There is no way she could have slept on it or anywhere else. Where and how did she sleep? I have no idea unless she just lay on top of the magazines. Where did she eat? Where did she sit? Under the largest table in the house are five non-working TV sets. Half a dozen non-working radios sit on top of the table. Did her neighbors dump things in her apartment? Did she bring them in from the trash? I'll never know. One room is full of free-standing industrial metal shelves filled with paint, paper (very good quality paper), brushes and other art supplies. Her drawings, sketches, and paintings lie strewn about. I pack away a few to take with me. The topper of all this mess is that in one unventilated corner of the apartment, old yellow newspapers are stacked from floor to ceiling. On a small table right next to the papers sits a can of turpentine and next to the turpentine a large box of kitchen matches. She could have burned down the whole building destroying herself and everyone in it.

There is one remarkable exception to all the mess. In a reasonable looking chest of drawers lie all of Mama's clothes folded perfectly with pink tissue paper lovingly placed between each garment. That chest of drawers is a little, carefully tended mausoleum. This apartment is a journey through Natalia's tormented mind.

Later I call her neighbors from the list she gave me and invite them to come in and see if they want any of her art. Some do, but most want the plastic, dollar store dishes. I ask some of them if they had been in the apartment before. They say "No" but knew Natalia as someone who walked around the neighborhood and engaged them in friendly conversation.

The next day Harry comes to help me. I look for but don't find the seven volumes of Proust. From a surviving small desk, we retrieve some photographs and some letters, including the love letter from Jess. For the rest, we bring in a cleaning service.

When I return home, I call her list of "friends." The friends are part of a life drawing class she regularly attended. I invite them to our house to sit Shiva. We live about an hour and a half from New York by train. None are willing to come. The art instructor who ran the life drawing class says that in a month there will be an art show by the class participants and maybe we can gather then. I call back her list of people and tell them we can have a simple gathering at the show in New York. They agree to it. The day arrives. Harry and I go to the location of the art show. It is in the basement of an apartment building. The drawings of the class hang in the dark space. But no one else is there except the instructor who organized the show, and no one else comes. We leave the wine and cheese we brought with the instructor and soon leave. Our Shiva is even more bleak and sad than Mama's funeral.

The experience still haunts me. I am sure Natalia would not have wanted a cremation. But she made no plans for burial, and there was no room for her in the cemetery where Mama lay buried in a plot next to Lenny, who also died. Natalia often spoke about her "friends" in New York, but clearly, she had none. I suspect some of the people from the neighborhood who she had on her list regarded her as a charming and friendly eccentric. Inside her apartment was a different story. There she lived out her rage, smashing furniture and living in an unbearable and dangerous mess. She could well have afforded help in the apartment and decent clothes but would not spend it. She lived on her Social Security payments in a rent-controlled apartment and stashed away most of the pension she received from her union. Her only indulgence was art supplies. Her work was mostly figure drawings. I found the body proportions distorted and disturbing; huge thighs and buttocks with bizarrely foreshortened legs. Clothed figures are of indeterminate sex often with clownish faces. I don't trust my judgment of them. I spent too many years frightened by Natalia's forceful physicality. Yet I have no doubt that she loved me and loved the family Harry and I made.

Did I love Natalia? She was generous and always ready to reach out to me. However, I felt no safety or comfort with her. There always seemed to be a low burn of rage just beneath the surface. She hid her violence and self-hatred when she could. And she preserved the evidence with the smashed furniture and the three-legged bed.

I was pleased that she always seemed interested in me and proud of me. As a child, I never looked to her as someone who could take care of me. Her comment about wanting to make her life worth a nickel seems saturated with sadness. I treasure her willingness to tell me the truth about John's sexuality. It helped me to see him as a man who suffered in his time and not just a dead beat. Possibly it was a way of telling me about her suffering and feelings of shame as well. Her pleasure in my family felt like a huge reward and appreciation for changing the three-generation repetition of our fatherless histories.

1943: Lenny

Lenny was fourteen when his father Marvin left the family. Occasionally he contemptuously referred to Marvin, as the "old man" as did Natalia.

Lenny and his wife Gloria never had children. I can imagine Lenny had no desire to take on fatherhood.

Lenny welcomed Mama's arrival in Miami Beach. However, he had not realized that I was coming too, that Mama had the nerve to arrive with yet another little sister in tow. I believe he hoped, now in his thirties, to have his mother to himself, finally free of the burdensome existence of his two younger sisters. He teased me mercilessly. The worst tortures usually followed something kind. For example, if we went to the beach on a day so hot the sand burnt my feet, he invited me to stand on his feet and hold onto him as we crossed the burning sand and entered the cooling ocean. But once in the water, he might dive under the waves and not emerge until I started to scream; or he might throw me over his head dropping me into deep water. When he saw me flailing and panicky, he laughed. In spite of my terror, I never complained to Mama. It was fascinating to have a male relative nearby. I was seduced by his moments of interest and kindness. And his body was so different than the women's bodies. Later I learned he was only 5'7, but to me, he seemed very tall. His shoulders were broad, and he had muscles. Later I thought he looked like Humphrey Bogart.

So when again he offered to "walk" me over the hot sand to the cool water, off I went for a frightening yet thrilling encore. He was a man so he stood for that missing piece in my life. It was enough to override being scared. However, he was mean to my mother, and so when she was around, I kept my distance from him.

He would not speak to my mother, not even "Hello" or "Goodbye." He avoided any eye contact with her, and if she talked to him, he turned his back. Later I learned it began when she married John. However, he shunned her even more after she divorced John.

Much later I learned from Mama that Lenny avoided my mother because he believed he was a Kohanim, a priestly class, honored by orthodox Jews and descended through the father's lineage from Aaron, the brother of Moses. Kohanim have certain religious privileges, such as offering the first blessing in a prayer service as well as restrictions that include avoiding any contact with both the dead and with the divorced. My mother not only married John who was only partly Jewish, but she also divorced him and so Lenny severed contact with her. Lenny did not attend a Synagogue, and I don't think he had had a Bar Mitzvah, but he believed he owned this paternal lineage and clung to it. Was this how Lenny kept in mind some aspect of his own father's existence and his connection to him? Was this how he filled the space of his father's empty place? Was this why he accepted not knowing about Mama's death or funeral until after it was over? Or were there other reasons Lenny avoided my mother?

When Lenny was sixty-five, he and his wife Gloria bought a trailer with a plan to "live like gypsies," free and on the road. They needed to run too. They saved up for their dream. Finally, they both retired and took off from Brooklyn, crossing the country slowly, arriving in Las Vegas. There, Gloria caught the gambling bug and within weeks gambled away their dream life. And so they needed jobs to cover basic expenses. They each took desk jobs and ended up living permanently in Las Vegas, rooted in a trailer park until the end of their lives—so much for running free.

I know nothing about their lives at the time of their deaths. Natalia kept some contact with Lenny. When he died of heart failure, Gloria immediately contacted Natalia to let her know. We did not hear about Gloria's death.

My Sister and My Brother

I never had a sister or a brother. At around age three or four, when I was in Nursery School in New York, I realized that other children had these amazing small relatives. They did not have to play by themselves when they were at home and so I invented a sister and called her Judy. Judy and I were about the same age. Maybe she was a little younger, but still, we were sisters. I could tell her what to do. We mostly played house. Sometimes I was the mother, and she was the baby or I was the baby. She was sometimes the father.

By the time we were in kindergarten Judy, and I often danced around the apartment and sang the songs we learned at school. As we grew older, we loved to listen to the radio before supper, especially Superman and Terry and the Pirates. If we were sick and stayed home from school, we loved soap operas, especially "Helen Trent". I wanted to send for the perfumed earrings Helen Trent advertised. I thought they would make a great present for our mother. I think they had a tiny compartment and in that tiny compartment, you placed a drop of your favorite perfume.

When our mother was home, she sometimes spoke to Judy. "Judy, would you like a banana?" "Judy, are you here in the bathtub with your sister?" Then she would set a place for Judy at the table. I always gave

Judy some of my food to eat. It was good to share with her because I did not have much of an appetite and neither did she.

When we began first grade Judy was very quiet. She only whispered and shared a seat with me. I don't think my teacher knew she was there. When I did play with other children in the schoolyard, I knew she would be waiting for me and I knew she would always come home with me. Judy came with me wherever we moved. Whether it was New York or Miami, whether our mother was around or away, Judy was with me.

When we were older, around seven years old, our mother went away for a very long time. Judy and I started a new game we called *journey in a covered wagon*.

Collecting together all our dolls and toy animals Judy and I sat together on a high chair—not a highchair but a chair that was high off the ground. A team of horses pulled our wagon forward. We rode out across the country to meet up with our mother. Because we would be away for such a long time, we always carried pimento cream cheese sandwiches on fluffy white Tip Top bread. I asked Mama, our grandmother, to make them and put them into a brown paper bag. I knew she would be happy to because Mama was always thrilled if I wanted to eat anything. And if Judy didn't eat her sandwich, I ate hers too.

We loved driving across the plains and over mountains. It was so peaceful. At night we fed the horses, set up camp, then we cooked over the campfire and talked about our day on the road, about all we saw and where we were going. But best of all we talked about finally seeing our mother again. "We'll all be so happy to be together again. She'll pick us both up and spin us around. We'll meet in a sunny place, go on picnics and ride in boats."

Then as the campfire slowly died down Judy and I fell asleep under the stars. We knew about campfires and camping from listening to the Lone Ranger and Tom Mix on the radio. We still had to travel many miles before meeting our mother but we were on our way even if it took us many days.

When I was around eight years old, our mother sat down to speak with me. She sat close looking intently into my eyes. "Aren't you getting a little old to have an imaginary companion?" I couldn't believe what I was hearing. "Imaginary companion!" Judy is my sister, my friend. We help each other. We play with each other. We even read stories to each other. Other kids have sisters and brothers and I need one too!" After this, I became more silent about Judy, but I certainly did not give her up. Our mother was worried and occasionally asked if I still had Judy and somewhere I too wondered—maybe I am too old for a Judy.

The crisis came on my ninth birthday. My mother woke me up and in her brightest voice pointed to the end of my bed and said triumphantly, "Here's Judy!" There at the end of my bed was the ugliest thing ever. Sitting on my bed was a life-size rag doll with a stupid sewn on grin and red wool braids. I was horrified. "That's not Judy! That is an ugly, stupid doll. It is nothing like Judy. Judy is beautiful. Judy is alive, and I love her. That thing is dead" Then I pulled out the biggest weapon I could think of and yelled, "I am not an only child I am a lonely child." I started to cry, and so did my mother. It was new for me to make her cry. Mama could make her cry, but I always soothed her or tried to. Now I was making her sad. That scared me.

The big stupid doll stayed around. She never had a name. Sometimes I put rubber bands on the dolls feet and slipped its feet on top of my shoes so that we could dance around the house. My mother liked to see me do this and I was glad to see her smile.

Looking back over the years I can see that my mother often got rid of people. She got rid of my father. She made friends then stopped seeing them. But maybe that was because we moved so much. Back then I could not dare to think she might want to get rid of me, but she did want me to get rid of Judy. Her intolerance of people important to me would continue to be a pattern through the end of her life. She rejected some of my friends and mentors. She disapproved of Harry and finally and most painfully she rejected Harry's and my children, her only grandchildren.

The episode with Judy was the very beginning of my almost secret life and gave me some independence from my mother and the family turmoil.

I missed Judy. I needed to replace her but I had learned it was necessary to keep such things quiet. The situation called for secrecy and tactics and so I found Marc, perhaps partly inspired by E.B. White's, "Stuart Little". Marc became my brother. Because he was only about six inches tall I could easily keep him in my pocket. He and I looked alike. He also had brown eyes and brown hair. I was skinny but he was wiry and for his small size very strong. He was also a little older and a grade ahead of me at school. This was helpful because he could sit on my school desk, lean against my big eraser and help out—especially with math and spelling. Like Judy I could always count on him to show up when I needed him but when I did not need his help or was busy with something else he stayed quietly in my pocket. Through many years he remained a faithful companion. We didn't play together the way Judy and I played but we talked. He had some very good ideas about school projects. If I struggled with schoolwork, he sat by and encouraged me on. "You can do it!" he'd say.

Creating Marc, a boy, was the beginning of my exit from the girl's dormitory. He may have left my pocket when I began High School but he transformed to what I have come to call, "the boy inside" which I think about to this day. I feel he is an internal, androgynous, icon of resilience and strength when I need it. He is a problem solver, a good sport, competent and sensible. Sometimes I need to experience him more externally like wearing good attractive leather boots, and a black turtleneck or a flowing, man-tailored shirt preferably in black or some dark and subtle color like olive or wine or midnight blue. These garments can make me feel like a stronger woman and a little bit male.

During my days as a dancer, I wanted to be very strong and to leap and jump as high as men could leap and jump. I wanted the shape of my body to be a female body but also to be muscular, trim and wiry.

With age, my body is more like a gradually closing telescope. My spine and waist are settling into my hips. Wiry and muscular is gone. My edges are soft. Very few boots feel comfortable on my arthritic feet. I still buy a flowing, silky man-tailored shirt whenever I find one. And then I think about Marc.

1944: The Venetian Pool

Lenny was still in the army, stationed in Miami Beach so Mama and I returned the following year for the winter months. I attended the second semester of first grade at South Beach School. This move was another painful exile from my mother, but this time Mama and I made regular visits to her distant relatives, the Gruenbaum family. They were recent refugees from Vienna arriving in Miami Beach via Cuba. The family members, who all lived together, included an elderly mother and three unmarried adult children all in their forties, Max, Hannah, and Molly. Their father died before they left Vienna. I barely remember the oldest and only son Max but his two sisters; Hannah and Molly are still vivid to me.

When Mama and I visited, Molly always seemed delighted to see me. She offered to play dominoes and card games. Molly made herself my adult friend. She often took her canary out of his cage, allowing him to fly freely through the apartment then land on her shoulder or my finger. We took walks and chatted cheerfully while she pointed out and named the tropical trees and plants that grew wildly in the vacant lots near the family apartment. Miami Beach was still partially wild. Vacant lots were little plots of Everglades with the typical richly, heady Everglade smell of warm, decaying vegetation.

Molly dressed plainly, but she had a closet full of beautiful, very small, high heel shoes. Some were magical. She had one pair made of Lucite that looked like glass slippers. Another pair was bright red and shiny like the shoes that transported Dorothy home from Oz. She let me try them on, and they almost fit.

Although I had spent many hours with Molly during those months, I was surprised when I suddenly noticed that Molly and I were close to the same height. It was only then I realized that Molly was a tiny person with an enormous hunchback. At first, I could not believe it, maybe she just hunched over sometimes, but then I saw that it was, in fact, a deformity she bore. Maybe her tiny beautiful shoes were her way to feel beautiful. When I think of her now, I still remember how lively and playful she was. We were two small, lonely people delighting in each other. For me, Molly was a loving playmate. Perhaps for her, for a brief time, I was a child she wanted and would never have.

Hannah, Molly's sister, was also warm, full of life and showed interest in me. Unlike Molly, Hannah was a beauty, even glamorous. She was a master seamstress who designed and sold clothes she made to order. Max and Hannah were the wage earners for the family. Because she worked during the week, I did not see Hannah as often as I saw Molly, but like my mother, Hannah was available on weekends. Often she drove Mama and me to the Venetian Pool in Coral Gables.

From time to time nostalgia sends me online to look for images of the Venetian Pool. Created in 1924 from an enormous, abandoned limestone rock quarry, the pool is surrounded and shaded by palm and banyan trees as well as tropical plants, brilliant flowers and small Mediterranean style buildings with red tile roofs. Waterfalls, small grottos, and islands connected by stone bridges evoke a green Venetian lagoon. Memory is often unreliable, but I am always stunned to see the pool again in photographs. It is just as I remember it when I saw it for the first time as a six-year-old. Why is it still is so vivid? It always evokes warmth, buoyant support, embarrassment and a secret revealed?

When Hannah, Mama and I visited the Venation Pool, Mama did not swim but chose to sit by the pool. Hannah took me into the water. Experiences in the water with Lenny left me nervous. If my feet could not firmly touch the bottom, I was frightened, so Hannah carried me. I wrapped my arms and legs around her middle and felt safe. In this way, we moved freely around the pool exploring all its dazzling features. We went behind the waterfall's roaring cascade, then into the dark grottos, staying until our eyes grew accustomed to the darkness, then out to the sunlight and the brilliant, reflective green water surrounded by flowers and singing birds.

As we passed by Mama in her hat and sunglasses sitting under the shade of an umbrella, Hannah suddenly called out to her, "Look how she loves me!" Shame and sadness overcame me. Hannah was right. I did love her. I couldn't help it. But it was a secret, even from myself. I missed my mother terribly, and Hannah reminded me of her. Like my mother, Hannah was beautiful, and she also took me into the world on weekends. Was it ok if she was my Miami Beach mother? Was it ok to love her? Was I betraying my mother? At that time I wondered. Now I know that loving Hannah helped me to remember my mother even when I had the frightening experience of occasionally forgetting her face. Missing and yearning were still intense but more bearable because I had Hannah. My loving feelings were not held hostage to only one person. I could love someone new.

Remembering how I loved Hannah may have something to do with how I now want to understand the comment my father made in our one meeting, fifteen years later. "You must be in love, or you would not have tried to find me." I could love and yearn for someone other than my father or mother. Natalia, try as she might, could not leave Mama and permanently move on to someone new. She suffered a painful and imprisoning bond with Mama. My mother, with her many absences, may have been trying to break free of both Mama and me. Mother/daughter clinging is the family lodestone. You give in, or you rip yourself away.

As years passed we lost contact with Hannah, Molly and the Gruenbaum family but I remember them still, and so vividly. To me, through my child's eyes, they were as colorful as the landscape of the Venetian Pool. Hannah and Molly were rays of warmth, liveliness, and hope. They were Jewish refugees who lost vast parts of their pasts. They bore the pain then moved on to create new lives for themselves. But, when I think about them now, there is a shadowed side. They were three single adult siblings in their forties who, as far as I know, did not, or maybe could not move on to love others outside their family.

The story of the Venetian Pool also reveals that in spite of the many changes and interruptions during childhood, two constant and unbroken threads sustained me. First, I could count on Mama to show up, albeit in her often angry, sometimes loving, often withdrawn way. And second, my besotted affection for my mother, even in her absence, and sometimes by surrogate, was also constant and sustaining. I loved my mother when I most needed to. In the future, our tangled bond would tear and fray. I would move on, but never entirely. I know that tug is there because after Harry and I were married, and occasionally to this day, long after her death, in dreams she and Harry morph into each other. Such emotional work goes on and on.

Friends and Lovers

Now looking back I see that losing contact with the Gruenbaums' was typical of the way my family broke threads of connection to people, in fact often got rid of people. Natalia and Marion made friends and then abandoned them. This was partly because there were so many moves, changes, entrances, and exits. It was also because they often felt hurt or bored or critical.

Sometimes when the four of us, Natalia, Marion, Mama and I sat at dinner, it was not unusual to hear, especially from Natalia and Marion, how they no longer liked someone or disapproved of someone. Now when I think of these conversations, I can hear their disdainful tones. Someone may have worn the wrong colors together or mispronounced words or didn't return a phone call. One particularly daft comment came from Natalia when we were together doing laundry at a Laundromat. While looking at the rows of washing machines with clothes sloshing around in them, she turned to me saying, "Don't other people's clothes look shabby compared to ours?"

They did not like Lenny's wife and would go on and on about how "coarse" and "stupid" she was. She was however quite warm toward me and generous with her gifts although she relentlessly argued with Lenny, but who could blame her. However what Marion chose to criticize was, "She doesn't even bother to look in the mirror when she puts on her hat!"

Marion and Natalia were the uneducated, fatherless daughters of poor shtetl immigrants. They could have received an education at no cost through the City Colleges of New York. They could have taken classes at night. But somehow they didn't think it suited them to mix with poor immigrants and children of immigrants even though they were themselves children of immigrants. They could have discovered great teachers and excellent education. Marion and Natalia were well spoken, sounded educated and had no regional accents. Possibly they imitated movie actors. They were devoted moviegoers. Marion did have some theatre training. They both read a lot.

Mama had a Yiddish accent even though for most of her adult life she denied she was Jewish. Lenny had a Brooklyn accent.

Marion and Natalia were smart. And in their way, they aspired to be more accomplished. But they seemed to build themselves up by putting other people down then detaching. I suspect each in their way suffered deep shame about who they were. Marion especially tried to appear she came from the upper class and looked as though she might have been a debutante. Her hair and make-up were impeccable. She dressed well in clothes she either made herself or found at discount prices.

For a long time, Marion and Natalia's way of cutting off people also affected my ability to make friends. Gradually as I reached middle-school age, I did make friends, but when we moved onto high school, I didn't stay in touch even when friends reached out. I remember the friends I abandoned, their names, their parents and siblings and visits to their homes. I must have been envious of the lives they had, and I wanted.

In 6th grade, the teacher asked us to write an essay, "Imagine your life as a grown-up." I pictured being married with two children, a cat, and a dog. For me, this was a radical goal. Through high school and part of college I continued to have only tenuous bonds with people my age. I was not really a loner. I spent time talking and studying, even visiting with fellow students. I had crushes on boys and young men. I went on dates but did not recognize that relationships needed to be kept up and that it took attention and effort to sustain them. I put all my efforts, and passion into becoming a dancer and little else felt important. I had to grow up first before having any on-going relationships outside the family. The one exception is Harry, my husband now of over fifty years. We met when I was twenty, and he was twenty-three. More than anyone else he showed me what it means to abide for the long haul.

Ongoing friendships with women began after Harry and I were married for several years. First, we formed friendships with other couples Harry already knew. It was not until my early thirties when we began to raise our children that my deeply held, permanent friendships with other women began to form. Sharing the ecstasies and agonies of marriage and raising children formed deep and lasting bonds. Initially, I looked to my friends and fellow mothers as models for raising children. The best of them and the ones I grew to love the most are the women who enjoyed their children, could play with them as well as regularly show up and be so reliable that their children barely gave a thought to their permanence. These mothers and fathers too were their children's predictable and familiar landscape. For me, Harry, our children, and these couples, now our oldest and dearest friends are my late forming bedrock, the place I return to, home. From them, I learned that friends, spouses, and children all require desire, tolerance, and devotion.

In my forties and fifties, as our children grew older and finally left home, and as I became more deeply involved in professional life, I began to make new and sustaining friendships with colleagues.

Not long ago a good and long-term friend commented, "If we got rid of our friends because they did something we don't like, we would have no friends."

I remain amazed that I now have this continuity at home and away from home. The swampy terrain that lies under my bedrock comes back in occasional moods, sometimes sadness but always first anger. I remember Mama's anger. I now know my anger/sadness covers fear, especially fear of losing someone or some part of myself. Also, I have repetitive dreams of being lost, trying to get home through dark, serpentine and deserted city streets. They all curve so I cannot see ahead. I wake up panicky and then feel relieved it is a dream. I know my way home now, but it took a long time to get here.

1945: Winter Journey

The end of World War II in September 1945 brought several changes in our family's living situation. Mama and I returned to New York from Miami Beach and remained there through the entire school year where I began second grade at P.S. 59. Around November or December of that same year, my mother decided to leave New York and move to Miami where she found a job as a secretary at a newspaper and also found Sean, a new lover. Natalia moved from New York to Palm Beach, Florida where she lived with Jess, a woman, and fellow artist. Lenny, when he finished his stint in the army, moved back to Brooklyn, re-joining his wife, Gloria. The only way I can understand these shifting arrangements is that Mama wanted to be near Lenny in New York and Natalia and my mother wanted to live separately from Mama so they could pursue their love lives privately. So Mama and I were alone together for the entire winter and part of spring.

That winter, Mama, now fifty-seven years old, became a mad woman. We were stuck in the apartment for some understandable reasons. We both had flu, and I had mumps. But then Mama sprained her ankle and lost her senses. She refused to get help. Instead, she confined herself and me to the house for many weeks while she hobbled around the

107

apartment using two suitcases as makeshift crutches. Too miserable to put in her false teeth, she hunched over the suitcases, grabbing the handles and sliding them forward while she did a pathetic little hop on her good foot. She looked like the village crazy crone or the witch from Snow White.

Mama called the local Gristede's grocery to deliver our food and then clung onto the kitchen sink to cook our meals. She asked no one to bring me to school. I must have missed many weeks of school. Apparently, the school never intervened. Maybe they gave up on me or thought we must have moved again.

Once Mama was off the suitcases and able to limp around she occasionally became enraged at me. I probably had "talked back" in some petulant or whiny way, saying something like, "No, I won't eat that. You eat it." Then she'd go to the closet to "get the belt." She claimed she always looked for the softest belt, but then would switch it back and forth at my feet screaming, "dance, dance!" It was humiliating. It is hard to believe now, but I could not feel my fury at her for doing this. I could only feel I did something horrible; I deserved it and had to win back her affection.

I certainly would not have been able to think that at the time. What I held in mind was, my mother waited for me somewhere in the future illuminated by my belief that she truly loved me and I loved her. Mama was just in charge of me for the time being. I am not even sure I thought out that much. At that age, I still didn't have many situations where I could compare my family to other families. Maybe I thought, or more likely felt, "This is how it is, and she is in charge so she must know." Once at a calm moment I was sitting next to her, she turned suddenly, and I flinched reflexively. I must have thought she was about to hit me. She was horrified to see me flinch. I do clearly remember being secretly pleased, maybe delighted, that she was so upset with herself. Only in retrospect can I see that Mama was probably insane at times during that wretched isolated winter.

She was often silent and needed to "rest" which she did for long periods every day lying in bed on her back, her arms tightly at her sides, her eyes open or closed.

The war in Europe ended in May, and still, there was and would be no word of her family's fate. Those letters on tissue-thin, blue paper that always began, "Liebe Fannie" no longer arrived. Occasionally Mama's sister Rivka/Rima visited. They spoke about their lost family in hushed tones. If Mama spat out "Hitler" or "Schweinhund", the tone of her voice sounded similar to when she spat out Marvin or John. Rivka/Rima would soon leave for Palestine where she too would die quickly of leukemia.

When I think back to that awful time I tend to compare it in misery to The Green Grass School, both times I felt lonely and trapped. But with Mama, at least I was in a familiar place with my familiar toys and the radio. But Mama herself was terrifying—her panic, her fury, her grief.

The isolation was the worst part of that winter. Why didn't she ask Lenny for help? She never asked Lenny for anything, and it didn't occur to him to step up. She could have asked Rivka/ Rima too. But she didn't.

I often stared out of the window to watch people on their way to and from work and school. We lived across the street from St, John's Church on First Avenue. In the morning boys and girls lined up in separate files to enter the Church's school building. In fall and spring, they stood like an army in their uniforms. In cold weather, they hunched into their coat collars to find a bit of warmth against the damp New York chill. In the afternoon mothers and sometimes fathers showed up to take their children home.

My mother gave me some good toys, and these helped during long lonely days. With my dollhouse, I imagined a family, a father and a mother pushing a baby in a carriage. Sometimes there was an older brother or sister. The little family was so enticing that I wanted to crawl into the dollhouse with them. Once I broke a little chair trying to sit on it. I was probably going mad as well. I remember looking at one of my books where the people lived in a little cottage. I stared so intently into this picture that I could feel myself sitting with the family at the small, tidy table eating bread and soup. With Tinker Toys I built bridges across chair backs and covering these with a sheet crawled into the cozy, translucent place beneath. Once, before my mother left, I listened to a record of Lily Pons singing Brahms Lullaby. I was so entranced with the soothing melody and the words I asked my mother to write them out so I could memorize the song. I sang it often. I re-read all my books, urgently listened to the radio; children's shows, soap operas, quiz shows, mystery, comedy and drama shows. Each week Life Magazine arrived. There was often a photographic essay on the War and also on the polio epidemic. I don't know what I thought of them. They were horrifying. Possibly they made my misery less significant. I can't be sure.

But most importantly I played the game I write about earlier, going on a journey with my imaginary sister/companion Judy. I played it over and over. It kept me more or less sane. When you are trapped, it helps to imagine you are on the move.

Finally, I did get back to school. One day there was a one-hour early dismissal. I knew it was to take place because we had been given a note to take home to our families. I had forgotten to give it to Mama and so stood in front of the school building as all the other children were picked up. Finally, I stood there alone. An older policeman came by wearing the big double-breasted coat with the metal buttons the police wore at the time. He asked me why I was alone, and I started to sob so intensely that I could not catch my breath. Finally, I was able to blurt out that my grandmother had not come to get me. Either I couldn't or wouldn't say that I forgot to give her the note. He looked at his watch and told me she would probably arrive at three o'clock—the usual time school let out. He took my hand, held it, and stayed with me through that whole hour while I continued to cry and cry and cry. Mama showed up at three o'clock very distressed by the scene and repeated over and over, "Thank-you, thank-you officer. I am so sorry. I'm so grateful." It is hard to know what was going on for me. As I look back, I wonder, "Did I set up this scene to in fact be as alone as I felt?" I think when that big policeman showed up and took care of me, my longing broke through the dikes and I dissolved. I also think it may have been an opportunity to let go and feel all that I felt. As I write this I think again of running across Sheep Meadow—let go!! At last!

But still, another visual detail of this episode keeps returning to mind. Did that policeman really wear a double-breasted coat with metal buttons? Is that a fictional part of my memory? Was I making the policeman into a conflated man/woman, a father/mother couple, taking care of me—briefly creating what I missed? Is that why I could let go and ride that wave of tears and sobs?

The next time I would sob like that was every Sunday with Harry during the first year of our marriage. I did not understand it then but perhaps, finally feeling safe I let go enough to feel the old sadness. Much later when I asked Harry how he withstood it, he said, ingenuously, "I thought all brides cried a lot." His experience taking care of a crying woman occurred when his father enlisted in W.W.II. His mother was moody and at times tearful and he, at age nine took it upon himself to explain to his younger brother and sister, "Mom is having her period." Who knows how any of the kids, including Harry, understood his explanation?

In 1989 I had another long episode of letting go and crying. I was in a good part of my life. Our son Matthew was in college, our daughter Sarah was a senior in high school. Harry was enjoying his work, and I was eager to begin my psychoanalysis and possibly train to be a psychoanalyst. I felt that I had made good choices and had the family I longed for. But how could this be true for me? Also, I was plagued by the fear that all I had and treasured, especially Harry and our children, would be destroyed by illness or accident. Another version of losing everything was that I would fall ill and slowly die.

I began psychoanalysis and to my surprise started to cry. I constantly cried for most of the first year and even into the second and third. I knew childhood had been troubling and difficult, but I still could not allow myself to know just how disturbing it was to live alone with Mama or be sent to The Green Grass School. After all, I survived, more than survived. I thought of myself as plucky, lucky and resilient and that I got through it all because first dance and then Harry saved my soul.

When I started psychoanalysis, along with Beethoven's late quartets, I was obsessed with listening to Schubert's Die Winterreise, a masterful German song cycle saturated with feelings of despair, longing, frenzy, and fury. The sound of the German language was familiar from hearing Mama speak German with Rivka/Rima. I must have listened to it scores of times sung by Dietrich Fischer-Dieskau. It is the sorrowful and solo journey of a rejected lover wandering through a bitterly cold winter landscape. The ice, the snow turning his dark hair white, his frozen tears, his rude awakening from a dream of spring confronts him with overwhelming loneliness, self-deceit, and defeat.

Schubert in his short life understood pain. Listening to his music helped to examine my childhood pain, especially the time I spent at the so-called Green Grass School or with Mama that winter of 1944-45 when she went mad with anguish and maybe began to acknowledge that her family in Europe had probably all perished. Sometimes I think of that time as the smoke from the Holocaust drifting into our building and creeping under the door into our apartment. Die Wintereisse was a way to remember my Winterreise of 1945, at a safe distance. Finally, in analysis, I could allow myself to know much more fully the sadness of those early years.

During that year, a woman in the neighborhood once asked me if I missed my mother. I realized then what the word miss meant. It was the slow, deep ache that moved from the middle of my stomach up into my throat. I often asked Mama. "How much longer until we see Mommy?" She might say, "at the end of the school year." or "three months" or "six weeks" and only when it was to be less than two weeks did I begin to feel hope and belief that I would ever see her again.

Once a week my mother wrote short newsy letters describing her life in Miami. She was having a good time meeting new people and enjoying the weather and the beach. When the letters arrived, Mama read them first then handed them to me. I believe my first impulse was to hold them to my face and breathe deeply. My mother also sent some photographs of herself in a bathing suit, stretching and smiling at the camera, looking happy and relaxed.

We joined her in late spring with a plan to live with her in Miami Beach.

1945: The Train from New York

I t is spring and the great day finally arrives. My daily journey by covered wagon to join my mother was about to become a reality. Out came the suitcases again but not for their recent purpose as crutches for a mad woman but to pack up our clothes. We were going to join my mother in Miami Beach—to go to her instead of from her, to live with her---at last!

Mama and I are standing in the Station. I tilt my head back to stare at the magical crystal dome. The last time we were here, was last November 1945 before the horrible winter of second grade. Mama and I did not board the train. My mother did. She was on her way to Miami to find a job and an apartment. She looked so beautiful that day wearing her purple coat with the fox fur lapels that flowed all the way down to the hem. We stood then, as now, under the great, glass dome, the noise of hurried travelers surrounding us. I clung to one fur lapel like a little monkey, pressing it to my lips and eyes, breathing it in. I wanted to inhale some part of her to stay with me. The fur was soon wet with my tears and sniffles, but I clung to it, deeply sinking my fingers into it.

My head came just above her belt. Her long, thin gloved hand patted me saying "Please, please don't cry." The conductor announced it is time to board. With me still clinging to her fur we walked to the train platform smelling of steam and old dust. She boarded the train, found her seat and waved to us from the window. I sobbed loudly. Mama begged, "Please, please don't cry. It makes it so hard for Mommy to leave." She said this with a stiff smile, hardly moving her lips while waving, trying to look cheerful. My mother's eyes, through the train window, were sad. She had the same stiff smile as Mama. I kept wailing. A lady wearing a hat with a veil came over and opening her big purse took out a yellow packet of Chicklets gum and offered me one. I looked up at Mama. Was I allowed to take something to eat from someone I didn't know? Mama nods O.K. I took it and bit. The train pulled out. The sweetness of the Chicklet filled my mouth. Mama and I walked out of the station and rode the bus home.

But today at Penn Station it is a glorious and different day. Mama and I are boarding the train going toward my mother. And we will live with her.

Two weeks before today Mama felt better again and began to make preparations to go. She told me that the weather would be very hot. I would need a short haircut to keep cool. We went to Best and Company to the children's beauty salon. A man began to cut my hair. When he stopped Mama said "shorter." This happened twice more until I had a full view of my ear lobes. Then she said "fine". I hated it so short but years later while looking at a childhood photo of my mother taken around 1919 I saw she had worn the same hair cut. Perhaps over the months, Mama began to think of me as her child or maybe she thought I was my mother. There still were times I too had to remind myself who was whose mother.

But finally today we are again at Penn Station waiting to board the train and going to meet my mother.

Young soldiers and sailors hurry by, sweaty and breathless lugging huge duffle bags on their shoulders. They too are finally going home to the people they love.

Mama and I will ride out on the Eastern Seaboard train. It takes twenty-six hours, three meals and over night. This time we have a Pullman seat. On earlier trips we always went by coach.

Part of the preparation for this journey includes a bag of licorice sticks, three comic books; Little Lulu, Nancy and Super Man as well as a book of Margaret O'Brien paper dolls. Today it is no longer the pretend journey in the covered wagon—it is real. Tomorrow I will finally see my mother again. I cannot quite remember her face, but I am pretty sure I will recognize her when the time comes. I can remember very well what it feels like to lie down with my head in her lap. But I have some trouble thinking just how it feels different from putting my head on Mama's lap.

Mama prepared for the trip as well. She is dressed up in her one suit and is wearing her one piece of jewelry, a gold pin in the shape of ribbon tied in a bow. She also brought with her a worn out terrycloth towel for me to sit on so that the plush seats won't scratch the back of my legs. The conductor yells "All aboard!" The train starts to move and soon speeds along. I look out of the window and make up songs to catch the rhythm of the telephone wires speeding by or the constant heavy drone of the train wheels. I read each comic book over and over again. The ride is too swervy to cut out the Margaret O'Brien paper dolls but I look at them wistfully thinking that with my new short haircut it will be ages before I can again have long braids like Margaret.

A porter dressed in a starched white jacket comes down the aisle announcing the dining car is now open. I follow Mama through the train. She struggles to heave open the heavy car doors. There is a terrifying moment as we step across the tiny platform between each train car hearing the screeching wheels and gravel flying like a torrential, deathly river below us. Mama can barely lug open that door to get into the next car. Surely we are about to be sucked into the space between the cars and ground to bloody pulp. This happens four or five times until we finally reach the dining car. Once in the dining car we are in a heavenly, quiet carpeted room. There are rows of dining tables with thick white tablecloths, silver coffee, and tea servers, the smell of grilling meat and brewing coffee, the sounds of chatting voices and knives and forks gently tapping against plates. I can't believe all these calm people, happily eating their dinner have just gone through the same scary experience hauling open those heavy train car doors and stepping over that violent monster below. We are seated at a table and Mama, after looking at the red, leather-bound menu orders roast leg of lamb, saying to me, "This is the best thing to eat because it is easy to digest." The food arrives and I fasten onto the mint jelly. It arrives in a tiny silver cup. I have never eaten anything so beautiful. It is a soft, sweet, shimmering green jewel.

After our memorable meal, we take another terrifying journey back to our train car, now even more horrible because it is night and you can't see the flying, killing gravel below like great monster teeth snatching at our feet. When we finally arrive at our car again the porter asks if we want the berth to be made up. This is confusing. I know it isn't my birthday and for a moment I think he is suggesting a pretend birthday party. Mama says "yes," and he begins to pull things down from the wall. Snow-white pillows and thick green blankets flow forth. There is a banging, and a whooshing as the double-decker bed falls into place. Then a sharp tug and the whole thing is covered with a heavy green curtain. The porter shows Mama how to snap the curtain into place on the top deck so that, "The little one won't fall out if she wants to sleep up there." He lifts me into the tiny room of the top deck. There is a little

117

lamp on the wall that casts a warm, gentle glow and a small hammock he says is to hold my "things." The little space is like the cottage of a tiny person who lives on the edge of the forest and welcomes travelers who wish to spend a safe night. I feel as though I have finally crept into one of my storybooks. I undress, slip into my nightgown and wiggle down under the crispy, white sheets. I turn out the light and try to sleep, but suddenly I remember crossing from one train car to another and I want Mama. I call to her, and she pokes her hand up through the green material that snaps me in. I hold her hand for a moment. She has soft, warm, fleshy palms and her hands smell almondy of Jergens lotion. I tell her "I can't sleep." and she tells me, "Look out of the window." I say, "There is no window up here." She says, "Come down with me." Her little compartment is a bit bigger than mine. The moon shines in, and I tuck myself down into her lap under the blankets and fall asleep.

It is morning. I am beside myself with excitement. By afternoon I will be hugging my mother again. The only thing now that distracts me is to look out the window at the Georgia landscape. Along the tracks, I see the dusty red earth. Dotting the land are brown wood or tin shacks slumping exhaustedly onto the ground. Black families sit on their sagging porches or stand by the train tracks staring widely and blankly at the passing train. A few small children wave and run along the moving train trying to keep up with it. I wave back to them.

When Mama and I once again make our harrowing trip to the dining car, I am enough used to it to notice that the air is warmer and smells like Christmas trees.

A few more hours and the conductor strides through announcing the train will be pulling into Miami in one hour. Mama gathers together some of our clothes, and we both go into the ladies room to get dressed. She bought me a new red dress with red socks to match. The dress is far too long. It hangs below my knees. My mother always shortened new dresses and bought me only white socks. But in the store, Mama insisted these looked best. And now she insists I wear the dress and socks. She quickly combs my very short hair and then dresses herself in a summer dress while I sit on a small vanity stool fidgeting impatiently.

It is now only ten minutes until the train arrives. Mama asks if I want to keep the comic books or leave them for another child. I tell her to leave the comic books, but I want the Margaret O'Brien paper dolls. The suitcases are all re-packed, and we stand close to the door as the train finally, heavily and with a huge lurch stops. The doors are noisily hauled open. The conductor jumps down and sets out a little yellow stool to step down on. The light is brilliant and golden. A billowy wave of sweet-smelling heat wraps around me. I feel the hot air on my bare legs. I blink in the sunlight and for a moment can only see shadow forms ahead. Then suddenly there is my mother. She swoops me to her, and I press my face against her skin. She is smooth, tan and smells like coconut and ocean water. She wears a sundress. As she holds me, I reach up to press my hands along her warm bare back. I try to impress the memory of her flesh into my hands so that I will never forget it again.

In a cab, we ride to her apartment, now our apartment in Miami Beach. In the dining area are several cases of beer and Coke. The night before we arrived she had planned to have a party with all her new friends from her job and others that she met during those long winter and spring months. But she had to call it off because she had a migraine headache and couldn't go through with it. Her party is over now, and mine begins.

119

PART III

JOINING THE WORLD—
COMINGS AND GOINGS

1947: Miami—Telephone 32293

At three o'clock today Mama picked me up from my new school and brought me home to our new apartment. Last year after leaving New York and second grade the three of us lived in Miami Beach, and I went to third grade at Central Beach School for the whole year. But now I'm in fourth Grade at Coral Way School, and we live in Miami. I'm in Mrs. Steven's class.

I drop my books on the kitchen table and rush to the phone to dial 32293. I hear Mommy's voice, "Miami Tribune, Mr. Palmer's secretary." Since Mama and I moved to Florida to live with Mommy again, I can call her every day after school and talk to her at her work. All I have to do is dial 32293. It rings only once or twice and there she is! Sometimes the line is busy, but that still means she is there and I try her again in a few minutes.

"Hi Mommy, it's me."

"Hi Sweetie, how was school"?

"Mrs. Stevens went out of the room for a little while, and the class got noisy. When she came back, she said she was very cross with the whole class. She didn't even care who was noisy and who was quiet, so she said we all had to do ten extra long divisions for homework. I am so mad because I wanted to play outside with the kids and now I'll be stuck inside doing long division."

Now that Mama and I live with Mommy again I can go out and play with other children. Mommy tells Mama it is ok for me to go out.

"Well, when you finish the long division you'll have a surprise. I'm bringing home three books from the children's book review editor. She reviewed them and thought you'd like these. She is very interested to know what you think of them."

"What are they about?"

"It's a series of stories about girls and boys from other countries. There's one about Mexico, one about China and one about India. They look good and have beautiful illustrations."

Everyone at Mommy's work knows me because sometimes if Mama and I are downtown, we stop in to visit. Once Mommy took me to her job, and I stayed there all day playing with a typewriter. Now they can all know Mommy has a daughter. Here in Miami, she doesn't have to pretend she has no children the way she had to in New York.

The book review editor and the music review editor give her children's books and records to bring home to me after they review them. I have a big collection now. I guess they don't have children of their own. I love the books and records, especially two records, one is "The Twelve Dancing Princesses," and the other is "Peter Church Mouse". They are stories and songs, and I now know all the songs.

Then I ask her,

"When will you be home? "Oh, gee I forgot! Not until late. Sean is picking me up from work, and we're going out. I'll put the books at the end of your bed, and you'll find them when you wake up in the morning."

"Oh, I thought you'd be home tonight because you were out last night."

"Right, I had to work late yesterday. Mr. Palmer needed me to get out some letters for him, so Sean and I are going out tonight instead. Let me talk to Mama, please. I'll see you in the morning, Sweetie."

I call Mama to the phone and slump into the chair at the table. A few minutes pass. I hear Mama say on the phone, "But I bought lamb chops to cook because I know you like them. What am I supposed to do with them?" I think to myself, "I'd rather have Mommy home tonight than have those stupid books." I take a pencil out of my pencil case, swallow the lump in my throat and start on the long division

Sean is Mommy's new friend. I once called him "your boyfriend." She told me not to call him that but to call him her friend. I said to her that when the girls at school like a boy they sometimes call him their boyfriend. She said I was not to say "boyfriend", even if I have a friend who is a boy. I don't understand why it's wrong, but I'll try not to say it.

Mommy looks happy when she's with Sean. They go out alone together during the week. Sean is a policeman. He doesn't wear a police uniform, but he drives a car that says, "Miami Police". Sean has a twin brother named Liam. Liam is married and has three children, two little girls, Ella and Anna and a boy Danny who, like me, is nine years old. Since I came to Florida, Sean likes to bring Danny and me along on weekends when he goes out during the day with Mommy. When we're all together, we look like a normal family. I like Sean. Sometimes we go to the beach. Sometimes we go fishing or to the Seminole Indian Village and watch the monkeys or the alligator wrestle. I especially like the alligator wrestle. That's when a man and an alligator wrestle and the man rubs the alligator's stomach until the alligator falls asleep. We also go to fairs and performances at Danny's school. Danny goes to a Catholic school. Mommy once called our weekend adventures "playing house". I hope she likes, "playing house". I love it. Maybe if she and Sean got married to each other, she would stay at home more at night and maybe even during the day too. And maybe she would have a baby. I would love to be a big sister.

Since coming to Florida, we've moved a lot. I don't mind as long as Mama, and I live with Mommy. A lot of soldiers came home from the war now. There aren't enough apartments in Miami until they build some more. So if you are not a soldier or the family of a soldier who died, you can rent an apartment for only three months at a time. Last year when I was in third grade we had to move every three months, but I was able to stay in the same school, Central Beach School, for all of the third grade and I joined a Brownie troop I liked it a lot. Some of the girls in the troop were also in my class at school. My teacher was Miss Carpenter. She was very jolly. I liked her, and she liked me too. She has a twin sister who teaches fourth grade. I did not get to have the other Miss Carpenter in fourth grade because we moved from Miami Beach to Miami. I don't like Mrs. Stevens nearly as much as I liked the two Miss Carpenters. Mrs. Stevens does not smile much, and she told me that I changed schools too many times. I wish I could have stayed at Central Beach, but two good things are that Mama and I are living with Mommy and we now have a year lease on this new apartment.

The apartments we live in are called "furnished". They don't have much furniture in them. Oh, they have beds and a table and chairs for eating. There's usually only one comfy chair with one lamp for reading. Mama gets to sit in that chair at night, and when Mommy is home, she and I sit outside on the patio where we can read until it gets dark. Then as it gets dark and cooler other people who live in the apartment building come out to the patio. They talk. I like to listen to them talk. They are mostly old, and they talk about their families and grandchildren.

One time last year when it was time to move again I went to school in the morning and didn't know where we'd sleep that night. Mama and Mommy both picked me up after school that day. Mommy didn't go to work because she and Mama spent the day finding our new apartment. They found one near my school. Before going home, we went to Broadway Joe's for an early supper and had ice cream sodas for dessert. What a treat! After supper, we came home. I liked the new place a lot because instead of a couch there was a porch "glider" in the living room. I loved it and rode it all the time for the three months we lived there. Mommy didn't like it. She said it made her seasick.

Mommy and Mama complained about having to move so much. It doesn't bother me. In spite of all the changes, it's mostly a happy time for me. I'm very glad to go to school every day, even if Mrs. Stevens is a grouch. In second grade in New York, I missed a lot of school. Most of all I'm very, very happy to have Mommy living with us. The fourth time we moved last year was different. Mama and Mommy couldn't find an apartment, so we moved into a boarding house with "kitchen privileges". Mrs. Howe was the owner, and she was very, very fat. She always wanted to hug me. She'd grab me and hold me against her big soft belly. It was like drowning in pudding. It got so that when I heard her loud, flapping slippers coming down the hall, I made a fast getaway. That was one place I was very glad to leave.

Even though I don't like Coral Way School as much as I liked Central Beach I joined another Brownie troop, and I really like the leader who is the mother of one of the girls. I wish Mommy could be our Brownie troop leader. She can't because she has to go to work. Maybe if she marries Sean, she could be a scout leader of my troop. We are getting ready to "fly-up" and become Girl Scouts next year when we're in fifth grade.

Mrs. Stevens was absent for a long time, and we had a man substitute teacher. He was a soldier in the war. I liked him a lot. He was very kind, never got mad at the kids and he was very handsome. One day while I was standing in line I was swinging my pocketbook and accidentally hit him with it. I felt terrible, and I kept saying, "I'm sorry, I'm sorry!" He knelt down and looked right in my eyes and said, "I know you didn't mean it. It was an accident; it is ok, don't worry." I started to cry. I don't know why. I understood very well that he was not at all mad at me. He was just so nice and so handsome. He had big shoulders, and his eyes were blue.

1947: Miami—The Rheingold Maidens

I have a friend who lives across the street. We're in the same fourth-grade class. Her name is Terry-Jo Jackson. I visit her, and we play mostly outside or in her garage. Her name is Terry-Jo because her father's name is Terry and her uncle's name is Joe, and her parents made two men's names into one girl's name.

Today we will work on a special art project. Her father and her Uncle Joe are Rheingold Beer salesmen, and they brought home for her a life-size cardboard stand up poster of the new Rheingold Maidens. One will soon win the title of Miss Rheingold, 1947.

I enter her garage where the poster stands taller than we are. The Maidens are all wearing the same pretty dresses. They are as tall as our mothers. They are beautiful now but we are going to make them even more beautiful. We each have a box of 64 Crayolas that includes a silver Crayola and a gold Crayola. So we will give them some lovely jewelry. We also plan to add some make-up to their faces. Terry-Jo brings in two milk crates so that we can easily reach their faces. First, we decide who is the most beautiful. I chose a maiden with dark brown hair as the most beautiful and who is sure to win the contest and she choses one with red hair to win. Her mother has red hair and mine has dark brown hair. These are our different first choices for the prettiest, but we agree on all the others and rank them in the same order. We give them all earrings and bracelets. We add more shades of red to their lips and we draw on extra long eyelashes as well as some beauty marks. We stand back to admire our work. But then we start adding silly hats and eyeglasses and then mustaches and finally long beards and big pointy teeth. We're working very hard and we're giggling very hard when Terry-Jo suddenly says to me, "Where's your Dad? I've never seen your Dad." I am drawing a tall black witches hat on the dark-haired maiden. "He's dead," I say. "Oh!" she says, "Was he killed in the war like Jimmy's father?" Jimmy is a boy in our class. "Mmmmm…" I murmur. Then I say, "Look at the tattoo I put on the blond one. It's a heart with an arrow and the words; I will love you always." She points out an ankle bracelet she just drew on the red-haired maiden.

I Said, "He's Dead."

"He's dead", why did I say, "He's dead"? When I think about it now, I'm ashamed of it. Back then, in 1947, I was worried and nervous.

When World War II ended in May 1945 Mama and I were still living in New York. The radio was on, and the announcer excitedly described all the celebrations in the streets. I was playing with Tinker Toys, laying the connected sticks between two wooden chair backs. Husbands and fathers were coming home to their wives and children. Mine wasn't. Our family was about missing fathers and husbands who never came home. I hung a sheet over the two chairs, crawled into the enclosure and curled up into the tiniest ball I could make.

Terry-Jo's father returned from fighting in the war. He survived gunfire and came home to Terry-Jo and her mother. Her Uncle Joe, a bachelor, also moved in with them. They all lived together in a new house they built themselves. Later her little brother was born. Terry-Joe was normal. She had a family with a mother and a father and a brother who lived together, with room for her uncle too. Her father thought about her and brought her the big cardboard poster of the Rheingold Maidens because he knew she would like it. Yet Terry-Joe lived through the war without her father. Not every father returned. There were boys and girls at my school whose fathers' did not return because they were missing in action or killed. At school, we were told to be especially kind to them. They were "…having a hard time." If your father was in the war, if he was missing in action or if he was dead, it was a new normal. It was a new normal to live with only your mother and often other relatives as well. But if the fathers lived, they eventually came home.

But a living father who didn't come home—that was not normal. What was wrong with my father? Did he ever think about us? Did he ever care about us? What was wrong with my mother and with me? Were we ugly? Were we mean? Did we smell bad? Maybe John would have stayed in touch if I were a boy. Maybe he didn't want a child at all. He never sent me a birthday card. And why did my mother have to get rid of him so completely? She even got rid of pictures of him.

It is only now, as a married woman, who has raised children with her husband that I know that most parents, even if divorced, don't necessarily annihilate the existence of each other or their children; or at least they usually try not to.

When Terry-Jo asked, "Where is your Dad?" I said, "He's dead." As far as I knew he was alive. He went missing but not because of the war. My mother left him and said she wanted nothing to do with him. Why did he go along with it? Why did he agree to have nothing to do with either of us? Did he hate us? Was my mother so angry that he was afraid of her?

At the last visit with John, my mother and he screamed at each other. That moment is the only memory I have of them ever being together. John wore an army uniform. I had no idea what he did in the army at the time but later heard from my mother that he was an entertainer in the U.S.O. Apparently, he was soon discharged as "unfit for military service." She probably learned it from her lawyer when she arranged the divorce.

How was he unfit? Did he get drunk? Did he break the law? But maybe because I knew he had been in the Army, I thought I could make my story into a new normal story. I could have said, "My father is missing in action." which seemed true in a way, or I could say, "He was killed in the war." Instead, I said, "He's dead." and let others wonder if he died in the war. I don't know what I would have said if asked, "How did he die?" But why did I say, "He's dead"? It chills me now that I needed to murder him. I knew he was no hero and didn't want to convey that by, killed in action or missing in action. Saying "He's dead." was a way to seem normal. By this time, at nine years old I knew there was a huge missing piece from my life and also from my mother's life and from Mama's life. Fathers went missing, and nothing and no one filled their empty place. I still hoped that Sean might fill that space.

Soon after the conversation with Terry-Jo, My mother and I went to the movies. I don't remember the movie. I'd like to think it was "Life with Father". After, as we walked back to the apartment in the balmy Miami evening, I had to get what I said to Terry-Jo off my chest. Our conversation went something like this:

"Mommy, Terry-Jo asked me why she never sees Daddy."

"What did you say?'

"Well first I pretended I didn't hear her and then she asked me if he was dead."

"So what did you say to that?"

"I sort of said 'Yes".' Actually, she just asked me where Daddy was because she never sees him. I guess I said, "He's dead."

If my mother asked me why I said, "He's dead." I don't remember it. If she did ask me, I think I would have said, "I want to be normal like other kids. Some have fathers who died in the war."

Then she asked, "Did she ask you how he died?"

"No. Is it ok that I said that Daddy's dead?"

First, she took a breath, and we stopped walking for a moment. "Yes, I think it is ok. It sort of makes things simpler, doesn't it?"

But then she went on; "Maybe when we talk about him, you shouldn't call him Daddy anymore. Call him John."

Why would she have said that? "Maybe when we talk about him you shouldn't call him Daddy anymore. Call him John." When she spoke about her father, she didn't say "Marvin" (although Natalia did). She called him "Papa." But I was not to call my father "Daddy." It wasn't enough that I killed him off. I couldn't call him "Daddy" either. It was as though I never had a father at all. And I went along with it. I needed to please her. Who else was there?

Maybe she was embarrassed that her father deserted her. I was ashamed that my father was nowhere on the scene. I accepted what she said. Mostly I felt relieved when she said it was ok. I told Terry-Jo my father was dead. And I was relieved that when other kids asked me where my father was, I could say, "He's dead." and let that be it. That is probably shocking enough for most people to hear. They don't tend to ask what happened—at least not at first.

But how was it "simpler"? Were we back to when she wanted me to pretend we were sisters and Mama was our mother? If John wasn't Daddy, then who was he? When I think of this conversation, it almost seems dangerous to try to make sense of things. You can feel crazy trying to figure out what is a lie and what is true. And how do you keep them straight?

So that talk, on our way home from the movies, marked the time I was to call my father John when she and I talked about him but to the world outside he was to be my dead father. Was he to be her dead husband? I don't think so because I heard her tell people she was divorced, so maybe being divorced did not embarrass her. After all, a lot of famous movie actresses were divorced, even at that time. So why did she agree that it was ok for me to say he was dead? I wanted to say he was dead so I would not have to explain his absence by saying he doesn't want me. I don't know that I was glad to kill him off, but in a certain way I was relieved of public shame, but only in the short run. Probably my angry motive was, Why can't I be like other kids? My mother may have thought she was being supportive in going along with "He's dead." Now I know what I needed most was help, to tell the truth. Maybe she was too wounded by her own deserting father to help me with that. She had learned to lie. Now, I was learning also.

As much as I enjoyed having friends and being more a part of the world, which I could not do when Mama alone took care of me, joining others outside the family created challenges that I did not have to face in the enclosed and isolated life with Mama alone. Now, living with my mother, I could play with other children and had close up views of normal family life. There were fathers who came home at night and enjoyed their children. At that time I didn't know another child whose parents were divorced. I heard about divorced families, maybe on radio soap operas. They were called "broken homes". "Oh the poor child, she's from a broken home." The idea of being called a child from a broken home made me feel sad, even pathetic. Even in broken homes many children still saw their fathers. I didn't want to admit my home was broken or that my father didn't call or write.

Very likely I romanticized the families I visited. For all I knew Terry-Jo's father and uncle got drunk every night and beat up her mother. And who was the real father of that new baby boy? Was it really Terry-Jo's Dad? Was it her uncle?

Did I, in fact, live a more peaceful life than some of the families that I looked at with longing? But I did know that some fathers liked their daughters and thought about them. Terry-Jo's father knew she would like the Rheingold Maiden life-size poster and cared enough to haul it home for her. I still wanted normal, whatever normal was.

I made a deal to trade my shame that my father wanted nothing to do with me for long-term guilt and confusion. I smashed the Pote/pot, killing him off with a lie.

1947: Miami Magic—Keeping Us Safe

After dialing 32293 on the phone to reach my mother at her work, we talked for about five minutes. Then I asked her the crucial question, "When are you coming home?" If she said she and Sean were going out that night and would be home late, I felt sad, and I missed her, but I knew I would see her again the following morning. I believed Sean would keep her safe. He wouldn't let anything bad happen to his Marion. If she said she'd be home, "Around 5:30" I was thrilled at first. But then as 5:00 o'clock approached, the time she left the office, I was gripped by fear. I was not puzzled by why I was so terrified, I knew exactly why. Once she left the office, dialing 32293 would not reach her. I had to stay as calm as I could and talk myself through it. And I had to keep her safe.

"Mommy said she'll leave the office at 5 o'clock. I know she'll walk to the bus stop, get on the bus, get off at 24th Road and walk the three blocks home. The whole trip takes half an hour. I love it when I hear her key in the door. It is a quarter to five now. I can do three long division problems before she leaves the office. I hate long division. We have six of them to do tonight but I can only do three now, and by then it will be five o'clock.

Ok, they are done, and now I have to get her home safely. I'll do what I always do. So far it has worked. She got home each time.

I'll sit exactly in the center of the couch right in the middle over the place where the two separate cushions meet. Now I'll sit perfectly still and read Life Magazine. Sometimes I wonder if it really works. But I'm afraid to stop because what if it really does work? So far she has always come back. But sometimes she is late. Then I get so scared that something bad happened to her on the way home. What if, as she walked to the bus, a car hit her? What if the bus crashes and she is killed? What if she is kidnapped or murdered in the street? If I knew she was with Sean I would not be so worried. Once I know she has left the office, there is no way to know if she is safe until I hear her key and she walks in the door.

Here is a new Life Magazine. It just came today. I can put the old one from last week away and now start the new one. Oh, here are pictures about the polio epidemic. The children here are in iron lungs. They can't move at all when they have polio. They can't even breathe, and the iron lung helps them breathe. Sometimes polio is called infantile paralysis. Here they are in the pool with a helper for exercise. I guess they can be in the pool when they can breathe again.

Billy who lived in this apartment building got polio, and he died. Mommy said it was because his mother let him go to the public swimming pool and he caught it there. Here are pictures of kids learning to walk. They have big metal braces on their legs. President Roosevelt had polio. I remember when he died. Mommy and Mama cried. What is the next story here? Oh, more photographs of survivors from the concentration camps. Most of the children died.

Rudy, a boy in my class, came from Poland. His parents died in a concentration camp. He lived because he was with nuns in an orphanage until his aunt, who stayed alive, picked him up. Poor Rudy, he doesn't have a mother or father. I'm lucky. I have a mother.

Oh dear, I reached the last page of Life. I'll go back to the beginning and turn the pages very slowly. Should I hold my breath like the children in the iron lungs? I can't. They would have breathed if they could have. So I'll breathe.

Oh! It is 5:30 already. Where is Mommy! She should be home by now! Is she still alive? Will I ever see her again? I'll count to four, four times. It will keep everyone in the family alive, Mama, Natalia, Mommy and me. I really don't worry about Mama and Natalia. But I shouldn't leave them out. It is just Mommy and me I worry about—mostly Mommy. But four is good because two times two is four. So four makes two extra strong. 1234—1234—1234---1234. No Mommy! No key in the door! It is a quarter to six. Where is she? Where can she be? I'll keep sitting perfectly still—right in the middle of the couch. I will look in four directions and make a square with my eyes and head. A square has four sides; like a safe place, all closed in. Start looking right, then look up, look left, look down, look right. Now the other way. Look left, look up, look right, look down. Look left.

Maybe the bus just ran out of gas, and that's why she is late. Maybe her boss had to get a letter out late, and she's taking shorthand and typing it up? But if that's it, and she knew she was going to be late, why doesn't she call?

Now I will be perfectly still in the middle. She's still isn't home! I just want my Mommy. Oh gee I'm crying now. That will make Mama get mad at Mommy. Mama has to put up with my crying. It is already six o'clock! Will I ever see her again!

Oh, oh what a terrible thought I just had. Rudy doesn't have to worry about his mother because she's already dead. If Mommy were dead I wouldn't have to worry about her. God will punish me for such a bad thought. I have to think of a worse thought to get rid of the bad thought. I want the atom bomb to drop on us. And then I will be dead. We will all be dead. No one will worry anymore. Oh God, forgive me. I just want Mommy to come home. There's the key in the door, Mommy!"

As miserable as I felt during these rituals they helped me actively do something to bear the pain that I could lose my mother as she alone crossed the war zone from 32293 to our apartment. And also to bear the pain of the fantasy that if I did lose her, the rest of my life would be nothing but a Winter Journey alone with Mama

When my mother finally arrived, she might have stopped for a quick drink with a friend or even with Sean. She could see that I was a shaky mess. Then Mama angrily let her have it for "traipsing and neglect." And then my mother would get angry with me for having "a tantrum" or for trying to control her comings and goings. "It's not your business! I'll be home when I get here!"

Once when I was overcome with a mixture of sorrow for being so upset and terror that I would lose her, in desperation, I said, "Please, please listen to what I need to say. It will save our lives!" In a fury and with sarcasm she said, "OK tell me what you have to say that's so important it will save our lives!" And I realized I had nothing to say.

Only when I was an adult could I wonder what this was like for my mother. She was thirty-four years old and finally, for more than six months, had lived in freedom while Mama and I stayed in New York for most of the winter and spring. Suddenly she had to again account for her life to her mother and nine-year-old child. She must have felt not only controlled but also imprisoned or at least on parole and expected to answer for all her actions. And she would be right. I did want to take control of her and of course, I couldn't. My fantasy of her treacherous journey home, dying on the way, was devastating. But if she did die, I would never have to worry about losing her again. I would no longer suffer over her preference to be out on a date rather than home with me. I had told Terry-Jo my father was dead. And I was killing off my mother as well.

Other ritual punishments to preserve my mother's life included needing to do a variety of things all in fours. Opening or closing a drawer or a door had to be done four times. But I also knew it was crazy, so if I was in someone else's sight, I was absolved of the repetitive action. But once alone, I owed my dues and had to perform the ritual of fours.

Sometimes after finishing my math homework, my least favorite homework, I had to rip it up and do it again. Also, I had to pray to God often for forgiveness because, to save my mother's life, sometimes I had to risk saying something cruel and outrageous, like "I love Hitler." I didn't have to say it to anyone in particular, but it had to be within hearing distance of someone. It could be a stranger. Then, under my breath, I would say it very fast. Was I love Hitler code for I love Daddy? Mama would be furious to hear, I love Daddy. I think it would have sent my mother to weeping. This all took a lot of time. It was exhausting. But those punishing rituals offered brief relief from fear and guilt.

Mama certainly had her punishing house cleaning rituals, lugging those heavy rugs to the roof and beating them, or walking all over the city to pay the bills or even succumbing to being my caretaker when she could have finally had time for herself. What was she beating herself for? Was it for surviving when her brothers and sisters died in the Holocaust? And why couldn't Natalia, at the end of her life even allow herself a place to sleep? The beat went on!

During the years in college, when I had separated from my mother but didn't yet know Harry, I felt free of the terror of losing someone I needed. But again after Harry and I married and even more so after we had children, I experienced similar panic about the possibility of losing them.

After we married, I had to learn to drive—a necessity for living outside New York. For years, over and over, I dreamt and dreamt again and again that I was driving the car and suddenly a man looms up in front of me. I hit and kill him. I awake in a panic. Was this a new edition of killing John, or imagining my mother killed on her way home and maybe killing off Harry so I would not have to worry about him any longer? The very thought sickens me. Are these the sort of tormenting thoughts that haunted Mama as she waited for word from her silent or silenced relatives?

The End of the Party

Through my ninth year, my mother, Mama and I continued to live in Florida. Natalia was living in Palm Beach with her partner and they occasionally visited.

I hoped my mother and Sean would marry. I liked playing house with Sean. I knew it was only playing but I loved the game and wanted it to be real. I began to suspect it was not to be. Now there were long serious phone calls between them. The family weekends stopped. My mother and Sean seemed to be breaking up. When I asked why she said Sean wanted to get married and if they did he expected her to become Catholic and to have more children. She was unwilling to do either. I wondered if she did not like Sean's interest in family outings with his nephew and me in tow. Perhaps she felt she lost some of his undivided attention. Maybe she wanted him for herself.

I remember going for a walk with Mama and my mother and dawdling behind them when suddenly I heard myself blurt out, "I wish I were never born!" My mother spun around yelling at me, "Don't you ever say that again!" Was my blurt-out too close to the bone—for both of us? I wanted her to marry Sean. I missed him.

One afternoon while she and I were walking home to the apartment I said to her that I wish she would get married, if not to Sean, to someone so we could be a normal family. I wanted to be like the families I now visited on radio and in the books I read—like Henry Aldrich and the Bobbsey Twins.

She was still occasionally seeing Sean alone when she received one of her calls from Irv. Irv Kahn was an old "friend" who occasionally pursued her. She saw him whenever she was in New York. He was forty-five years old and never married. Apparently now he was begging her to marry him. Mama was all for it. I suspect she had had enough of keeping tabs on her youngest daughter and being responsible for her grandchild. She was about to turn sixty years old.

And there was something else. I had the bare beginning of breast buds and they felt tender. I did not know what it was and showed it to Mama who treated it as something wrong. She put her "ointment" on them. Her "ointment" was boric acid ointment that once helped her when she had an irritated eye and so believed it to be a panacea for any and all physical ills. She convinced me I had something that should not be there. But Mama had both older and younger sisters and raised two daughters. I'm amazed she couldn't let herself recognize that this was a normal change for a girl my age. Now I suspect this was the first sign of my approaching teen years and she was terrified at the thought of having to deal with yet another wild teenage girl. Encouraging my mother to marry Irv, with the assumption that I would live with them, was her sudden new exit door. Also, Irv was Jewish. I remember her saying to my mother, "It is about time you chose a Jew."

That August the three of us returned to New York, and Natalia joined us. We all moved back into a one-bedroom apartment. In September I went to P.S. 59 for the first two months of 5th grade. This time my mother did not look for a job. She married Irv in October 1948. Then she and I moved with Irv to a new apartment located in Greenwich Village. I changed schools again to P.S. 41 for the remainder of the 5th grade. I barely knew Irv but was glad to leave Mama's care. I was also glad my mother would have a man to take care of her. When she was with a man her safety, even her life would not depend on my efforts at magic. Having my mother at home when I came home from school was a life long dream. Would the dream come true?

1948: New York— The China Doll

My mother and Irv married on Halloween, October 31st, 1948. Irv was a businessman who ran an import-export business and dealt mostly with Chinese objects. Mama was thrilled. "He is a nice respectable Jewish man, a good earner, not like John, that crazy, drunk, bohemian, sponge." I loved the idea of being a normal family.

Before his marriage to my mother, Irv lived in a hotel just off Times Square called "The Dixie." He said, "It's convenient. My room gets cleaned, and I eat in restaurants. I can spend a lot of time at the office." Just before the wedding, we visited him at The Dixie. The corridors smelled of cheap perfumed disinfectant. His room was simple; a double bed, a plain dresser and an upholstered chair that sent up a little cloud of gray dust when I bounced onto it. Out of the window and across the street were two neon signs. One advertised a men's steam room and a Turkish bathhouse. I think it was called something like "Luxor Baths." The other was a cocktail lounge. Maybe it was called, The "Rendezvous." I don't think Mama knew where Irv lived. If my mother thought it was shabby and strange, she said nothing. We just moved forward.

At the wedding, my mother did not wear the long, white gown I hoped she would. I wanted to see her float down the aisle looking like the bride on the wedding cake, but she told me, "That just isn't done at second weddings." She wore a silky, pink dress the color of seashells. It was very soft and flowing making her slim figure, her delicate face and fine skin look like a porcelain maker's masterpiece. Her brother Lenny, when he learned she was getting married to a Jewish man, agreed to give her away and escorted her down the aisle. Mama sat beside me and wept.

Irv had many Chinese friends and colleagues who came to the wedding. Among them, Mrs. Mai Shou and her daughter Chantelle. Mr. Shou had been a business colleague of Irv's who died recently of tuberculosis. Chantelle, about twenty years old, was a nightclub singer. She was unusually tall and robust for a young Asian woman, but her face had a dainty, painted look like the Chinese women on the calendars that hung in some Chinese restaurants. At the wedding party, Chantelle sang La Vie en Rose. She sang it to Irv, first in French and then in English with a bold delivery. Irv looked back at her with a broad, warm smile. He glowed in a way that I had not seen him glow before. We had a record of "La Vie en Rose" in both English and French so I learned the words in English and took to singing it for months afterward. I wanted to make Irv glow too. It didn't work.

Irv was the oldest of three, born to Yiddish speaking, Russian immigrant parents. He was his parent's favorite because, like his father, Chaim, Irv also was thought to be a successful businessman. Chaim was truly a self-made man. He had started the business selling novelty items from a pushcart on the Lower East Side. Chaim was so thrilled with "making it" in America that he made his wife promise always to keep French champagne in the "Frigidaire". He drank his glass of champagne every night with the supper she made for him. On Saturdays, when we sometimes came for lunch, I remember seeing the pre-prepared Sabbath meal in a pot sitting on the pilot light of the stove and on the table stood bottles of seltzer and French champagne. The champagne had to be opened by his Italian neighbor because opening a bottle was considered "work," and of course there was to be no work ever on the Sabbath, but there would always be champagne.

Irv's Chinese connection developed after the war. Apparently, he did all right as a businessman. My mother said, "I am glad to not worry about money." However, one thing puzzled me from the beginning. When they chose an apartment, they chose a one-bedroom apartment. When we moved in my mother insisted I take the bedroom and she made a big fuss about how lucky I was to now have my own room. She and Irv slept on a Castro Convertible couch in the living room. My room hardly felt like mine. Once while listening to the two of them argue, I heard Irv yell, "You didn't tell me she was coming too." He thought I would stay with Mama. Could my mother have actually known that Irv assumed I would stay with Mama? Could she really marry a man who didn't want me? I suspect then I couldn't allow myself to believe that she did. And if she did, maybe she refused to give into it and so brought me to live with them. I am sure I needed to believe my mother would do the right thing. That moment I may have given up hope of ever growing up with a father. But maybe Irv would take care of her and keep her safe.

Irv remained distant from me, but I wanted the appearance of a normal family. When I started going to a new school, I acted as though Irv was my father. I took up the family tradition of name changing and asked if I could use his last name as my own. Then all three of us could have the name Kahn. I did not want to be the only Pote. They both agreed. I don't know why they agreed. Again I believe it was a misguided effort to make things appear simpler than they were. I wanted to re-write my story. I amputated my father's and my name. I smashed the Pote/

pot again like I did when my friend asked, "Where is your Dad?" And I said, "He's dead."

My mother furnished the apartment and bought both of us new wardrobes. However, Irv forbade us to go to retail stores saying, "I have a friend in the business. He owes me a favor. Why pay retail?" At Irv's insistence, we were only allowed to shop "wholesale" at garment and furniture warehouses owned by some of his cronies. My mother called Irv "shrewd" a word that seemed vaguely insulting but also respectful of what she considered to be his clever wits. He operated his business and his life with an intricate network of favors. It was important to be owed favors. But more than that, it was crucial that he was owed more favors than he owed. The best situation for him was to be owed a favor and only call in the debt when he could be sure that the return favor would be equal to or less than the favor he had given. The favor he requested must at the very most neutralize the original debt. In this way, he carefully made sure that he had many favors he could call in and never be indebted to anyone else. How Irv calculated his favors, received and given, was his own mysterious, personal code of justice. He carried a little notebook in his breast pocket in which all of these negotiations were carefully tallied.

Irv met most of his business contacts, both Chinese and non-Chinese in Chinese restaurants. He seemed to have special relationships with the restaurant managers and owners. Most were recent immigrants. He told us that it was essential that he stay in touch with the Chinese community in New York because it was through them that he made his contacts in China when he went on buying trips to Hong Kong.

My mother and I often went to Chinese restaurants with Irv. We were usually invited to sit in the kitchen surrounded by the dripping Peking ducks that hung on a clothesline in every kitchen. I grew familiar with bird nest soup, moo goo gai pan, Peking duck, of course, lo mein, ancient eggs, winter melon, and sharks fin. I didn't really like the taste of any of these dishes but ordered them because I liked to say their names, especially moo goo gai pan. "I am embarrassed to see your almost full plate go back to the kitchen," Irv complained. Soon it became clear that eating in Chinese restaurants with Irv was not simply a slightly exotic adventure in our lives. It was, in fact, the only way to have dinner with Irv. No Chinese restaurant, no Irv. On evenings when we didn't go out with him, he returned home late, long after dinnertime. In fact, even on evenings that we ate out with him, more often than not, he took us home and then went "back to the office." In fact, the only place Irv ever went at night was, "back to the office." Even though I did not see much of him, I wanted to think of the new marriage, the new school and the new living situation as a new start.

On Saturday nights, if we went out with Irv, we had dinner at The China Doll. The China Doll was a nightclub that featured assorted acts all done by Chinese artists. There was a juggler, a tumbler, a magician, a fire-eater, a contortionist (my favorite) and Chantelle Shou who sang romantic "torch" songs in Chinese, French, and English. Chantelle did not receive the name Chantelle from her Chinese parents. She invented her new name as a teenager when she sang at the Mott Street Community Center talent shows. Her choice of name was influenced by her high school study of French. She was "discovered " by a family friend when he opened the nightclub. She had a fairly good voice but mostly a certain French chanteuse style with a bold delivery. She was a hit with the clientele, both Chinese and American businessmen.

At the China Doll, we sat at a stage-side table with Chantelle's aunt and uncle. Her uncle worked at the nightclub. His wife, a very quiet, traditional Chinese lady wore beautiful embroidered dresses with slits up the side. Also at the table were Chantelle's sister Helen (who renamed herself for Helen of Troy) and Mrs. Mai Shou, Chantelle's mother, now a widow in her mid-forties. Mrs. Shou was crazy about Irv. She brightened whenever he came into the room and treated him like the Grand Mandarin. Irv revelled in this. Only when we were with the Shou family did I see Irv smile and even laugh out loud.

During these outings my mother was stiff and formal, making tight, light conversation with the ladies. Having grown quite thin since her marriage, she looked and moved like a store manikin. She now always wore make-up, artfully applied to her fine-boned face and took special pains to have her hair done weekly at the beauty parlor. Her clothes were tailored and tasteful but with none of the Bohemian dash when she made many of her clothes.

One Saturday night, as I watched the contortionist wrap his legs around his neck, I glanced over at my mother who looked as though she might be ill. At first, I thought she was reacting to the show, but then I saw she was very pale and glassy-eyed. I realized she was crying. I took her hand. It felt small, bony and cold. As the show went on her eyes brimmed over with tears. She blinked them away when she saw me look at her. She smiled painfully and I was filled with a terrible worry and sadness for her. At home, Irv was never the beau vivant he was with his colleagues or with the Shou family. With us, he seemed afraid to laugh. He turned his face away if anything struck him remotely funny.

Irv and my mother began to argue at night after he came home "from the office." I could hear them from my room in the tiny apartment. Sometimes I opened the door a crack and watched. She cried and frantically grilled him with her questions. "Why are you so obsessed with all things Chinese?" "What do you do for so many hours at the office?" He would shrug and turn his back on her or pick up the newspaper and ignore her. As her fear turned to rage, her face contorted into a terrifying mask. Then everything really cracked open. Her shrill screams were like shattering glass. "You're no husband! You're nothing but a lump of dead wood. You just grow old; you've never grown up. You use this house like the Dixie Hotel, and you treat me like your maid. I think you're out screwing some whore. Or maybe it is so-called Chantelle. Is she your goddamn concubine, your high paid whore? Get out of here. Go back to The Dixie. Get out of here. Go screw your whore." When she accused Irv of Chantelle being his concubine, he bellowed at her, "Your crazy! She is the daughter of someone I did business with and who died. I am nothing but a good friend of the family. They respect me. You don't. All I am for you is a meal ticket so you don't have to have some stupid job that you can only keep if you flirt, or more than that, with the boss!" She screamed back again," I'm nothing to you but a pretty little Jewish face so you can look respectable, instead of looking like some weird pervert who lives at the Dixie."

Would Irv have preferred to marry Chantelle's mother or Chantelle? Chaim, his father, would never have agreed to it. He might have threatened to disinherit him if he married someone who wasn't Jewish.

The fights with my mother usually ended with Irv walking out and staying out for hours. Once, after I heard him slam the door, I went to my mother for comfort saying I was scared of what was happening. She responded, "You should not be interested in what is happening now. Pay no attention to it. You should only be interested in the results." This last sentence, "You should only be interested in the results." told me nothing of course except to not bother her with my worries.

After one of the fights between Marion and Irv, when I was not supposed to be interested in what was happening, Marion came into the bedroom where I was sequestered. She was both angry and crying. She picked up a plaster of Paris lamb, white with a painted blue ribbon around its neck, about three inches high. I won it in Coney Island after throwing a ball and knocking down some duckpins. Marion asked me,

"Can I throw this out the window? It will help me feel better." Of course, I said, "Yes." She pitched it hard out the window throwing it against a brick wall facing the building. It smashed to bits leaving a big white powdery spot on the wall. The spot remained until the next rainfall. She was indeed calmer after but must have also felt remorseful because she began to justify it urgently. "It gives me some relief and gives the man who cleans up downstairs a job to do which helps him to earn money." Even at the time, this last struck me as absurd. I believe I just as urgently tried to be the epitome of understanding. It was hard work to try to see it through her eyes.

The arguments with Irv, in one form or another, recurred many times. He somehow managed to placate her and things would calm down for a short time, only to erupt again. She was financially dependent on Irv. Maybe she felt trapped.

Irv was not generous with his money. He demanded my mother tell him everything she bought and also told her what to buy. He wanted her to have a Persian lamb coat, and he wanted her to wear it when she went out with him so that his business connections would think he was prosperous.

When she decided I should have ballet lessons she dutifully asked him if I could take them and he said, "No, it's unnecessary and too expensive!" She took the money from some other part of the budget and insisted I have the lessons, but I had to keep it a secret. I hated the classes, and I hated keeping the secret, and I was no good at ballet. I was nervous about it. What would Irv do if he found out? Then it all came to a head around bathing suits with little twirly skirts.

Summer was coming, and we went to a wholesale children's clothes warehouse where I tried on bathing suits. I fell in love with three different one-piece bathing suits that fit skintight on top and then flared out into little skirts. One was white with flowers. One was pink, and the third was aquamarine. I could not decide which one I wanted and my mother said, "let's get all of them." I was thrilled.

One day in June as we were getting ready to go to the beach I put on one of my three gorgeous bathing suits. She said, "You look like a ballerina. Twirl for me." I felt awkward, embarrassed and angry at her demand. All I could think of was the secret ballet lessons I hated. "No, I don't want to twirl!" I whined. She repeated, "Twirl for me!" Again I said, "No! I don't want to." She repeated it again adding, "That's the least you can do for me!" Then I yelled, "No, I won't twirl for you!" Then angrily she yelled back. "Then take off the bathing suit." I took it off, put on my clothes, and added the other two to the pile saying, "I don't want any of them!" I never wore them again. One sleepless night I went to her and said I don't like ballet and I don't like keeping it a secret. The classes stopped. The marriage went on—for a while.

There were more dinners at Chinese restaurant kitchens and more Saturdays at The China Doll. Chantelle always greeted Irv with a big warm hug. Maybe Irv was right; Chantelle was like a daughter to him. When she sang for him at the wedding, I knew he was special to her. I certainly wasn't special to him. He ignored me. I think he simply had decided that at forty-five he should have a wife. My mother, who was decorative and Jewish, filled the bill. They did not love each other. The marriage was doomed. Why didn't she realize before she married him what he was really like? I would have to keep worrying about her. There was no strong man to keep her safe for me.

I began to have a terrible time sleeping at night. Over and over I thought about my mother calling Irv a "lump of dead wood" and wondered what she meant. "A lump of dead wood" like a puppet? She was like a stiff puppet herself—or a china doll. Why did she marry him? How could she not know what he was like? How could she not know he didn't want me? This was the moment her beautiful porcelain began to crack. But I could not bear to know it then. Not yet.

Just before the 6th-grade summer recess she announced that I was to go away to summer camp. "You are so lucky, I wish I had had the advantages you have when I was your age. Thanks to Irv you are going away to summer camp this year." She stood in the doorway of the bedroom where I was struggling with my math homework. For the first time, I found schoolwork difficult. My grades were plummeting. She was very upbeat. "I wish I had had such a great opportunity when I was a girl." She went on. "It is a sleep-away camp. You'll be able to go for all of July and August. Isn't that exciting." I heard her words, all said in her normal voice, but they assaulted me like a barking dog. Was this exile a new edition of The Green Grass School? At that moment I couldn't allow myself the question. Unthinkable.

The camp colors were green and white. We went on a special shopping trip for the camp uniform. There were four pairs of green shorts, four tee shirts with the camp name, Wonder Trails printed in green across the chest, two bathing suits (new plain ones), sneakers, one pair of long green pants, one camp sweater, a canteen, and a flashlight. I liked the canteen and flashlight. My mother ordered nametags and sewed them into my clothes.

I suspect summer camp for me was planned, so she and Irv could see if they might do better without me on the marital scene and if they did better, was the next step to send me back to live with Mama?

1950: Camp and the Dancer—Camp

American troops were in Korea. Life Magazine showed many photos of miserable young Marines huddled in a frozen and bleak landscape. I suspect my expression matched theirs.

The day for leaving arrives. We meet the camp group at Penn Station. Within a few hours, we arrive in the Catskills. The campsite is a big field with very few trees and a scatter of small wooden cabins. A flagpole stands in the center of everything. There is one big wooden building where the people who own the camp live. A large screened in porch serves as the mess hall. There is also an infirmary should anyone get sick. I am led to my cabin with other eleven and twelve-year-old girls. We are intermediates and are told that during the first week we have to come up with a name to call ourselves. I don't care what we call ourselves. I'm on a forced march going through the motions—lonely, homesick, scared. When we sit down to eat in the big eating porch full of strangers I am utterly miserable and can't eat, I start to cry. The "Camp Mother" an older woman is called over, and she takes me back to the cabin. She tells me, "Be brave. You have nothing to cry about. You're here to have a good time. Your parents sacrificed to send you to camp. The only girl in your cabin who has reason to be upset is Margaret because her father died this past year." I stop crying but every once in a while a sob escapes. The other girls come back. We are supposed to unpack our stuff and put it neatly on the wooden shelves above our cots. The cabin smells of old musty wood.

After days of weeping and moping I begin to hold it together and dutifully march through the camp routine; flag raising, volleyball, swim instruction, free swim, lunch, rest hour, softball, free swim and on and on. I am numb and leaden. The days pass. I get through the nights by lying like a mummy on my narrow camp cot. If I were at home, I would not be in bed. I would be listening to the radio, "Can You Top This?" or "Mr. Keen Tracer of Lost Persons." Daylight arrives. I march robotically through the activities. Volleyball, softball, swim, lunch, rest period, letter writing. I hate it all. I write a none-letter. "Dear Mommy and Irv. We had volleyball, softball, swim and lunch, arts and crafts—lanyards, swim, free time, supper, sing-along, lights out. Love, (I sign it) Me." At night, when everyone else sleeps, I wonder what is going on between my mother and Irv. I am at the mercy of my guesses.

Camp and the Dancer—
The Dancer

Then I meet Rachel. Rachel is the dance counselor. She arrived at camp late because she was dancing in a summer stock performance. Rachel is a sad, preoccupied and beautiful young woman with lovely long hair that she wears caught up in a bun. Because she is the dance counselor, she mostly wears black tights and a black leotard with a long swirly skirt that fits snugly over her slim hips then flares out in arcs as she moves and turns.

Tonight is counselors' talent night. I sit with my cabin mates on the long wooden benches in the rec hall. There is a line-up of lip syncs, parodies and skits spoofing the camp directors. The curtain closes and rises again on Rachel. She lies on her side with her back to the audience.

What happens next I could not have described it at that time. But what I saw, I felt with thunderous emotional and physical intensity. Only now and in memory do I have words for it.

The music is a percussive wail, and Rachel's beautiful, sad face becomes all of her caught in a rhythmic swirl of driving convulsive motion and feeling. Her entire torso seems to sob as she spins and catapults from the floor piercing the air with explosive staccato leaps first arching backward now forward, grief turning from desperation to fury to protest. Her wild movements are held together by her technical skill, by the strange yet ordered music, and by the frame of the proscenium arch.

Her dance draws to a close as a thoughtful lament. She stands contained and calm at the close, not in a place of resolution, but as a woman newly informed by a full experience of her dark feelings. The curtain closes, and I feel the rising of my own deep sobs. I run from the recreation hall into the cool evening. My own storm of body-racking grief cracks the summer's brutal and suffocating heat.

I know now that Rachel's dance expressed my own despair and fury, feelings I couldn't yet name. She spoke another language, full of passion, powerful movement and precise skill, movements that mirrored my stifled, convulsive sobs and named my sorrow and isolation. Her dance spoke to me. It told me that I am not just an unhappy, homesick eleven-year-old crybaby but that I was living through a crisis. The pillars of my life were crumbling all over again. How would I get through it? Her dance also told me there was a way to take control of some of what I felt without telling myself I should not feel it, or as my mother said, "You should not be interested in what is happening now." I could do nothing about my mother's disastrous marriage. I could do nothing then about the fact that as a child I would never live in a normal family with a father, but Rachel showed me a way to feel it and live with it. I was angry with my mother for messing up our lives. I was ashamed of her poor choices. Her wrecked life at that time wrecked mine. She was miserable and too broken to bear my anger and sadness at her failures. I was angry with myself for failing to win Irv's interest let alone love. I felt that Sean really cared that I was on the scene. I would not go as far as believing he loved me, but he did love my mother and Irv did not.

Rachel's skillful movements conveyed despair, rage and defiance without words, words that then felt forbidden. But she showed me that dark feelings were not forbidden. Dance, the kind of dance she did, is a language—a language so much more expressive than the constraints of ballet. I wanted to speak it.

A New Language

Rachel's dance classes begin today. She says to our group, "Everyone, sit on the floor with your legs crossed. "Sit high on your sitting bones and breathe deeply. In, out, in, out." She shows us exercises to make us strong. We get up off the floor and first just walk as though we are proud of ourselves. Then walk as though we are carrying a heavy burden, then run like we are going toward something we love to do, like jumping into a beautiful lake—run as fast as we can. Now run like someone who wants to hurt you is chasing you. Every day that we dance in class with Rachel I feel lively and spirited again, even when we dance about sad or bad things. If I could have said it then I would say we moved, not from our limbs or muscles or joints but from our insides out.

Now it reminds me of those precious Saturday's when I was around five or six, and my mother took me out of Mama's small, overheated apartment into the big exciting world. We began with the zoo or the Museum of Natural History, then out for lunch, then ended each outing with a trip to Central Park's huge, open Sheep Meadow where she yelled, "Run!" I ran for my life and my spirit, consuming the ground under me, smelling the turf, feeling the wind at my back—flying!

It is the last week of camp. I know I'll miss Rachel. "Rachel," I ask, "Please tell me about your dancing. I want to dance too." She says to me "I'll be a senior at the High School of Performing Arts. The dance you saw me perform will be my senior project. I worked on it all year. What did you think of it?" I say, "I never saw anything like it. It made me cry but in a way that made me feel better. It made me want to dance like you. How did you get started?"

"Before going to Performing Arts, I studied at The Martha Graham School."

"Oh!" I say. "I know who Martha Graham is! She was the secret celebrity on my favorite radio quiz program "Truth or Consequences." She was "Miss Hush." She was called "Miss Hush" because she didn't speak. She danced. "Yes," Rachel says, " Martha Graham was Miss Hush."

I remembered the program well. It took eight weeks of riddles and clues for a call-in contestant to guess that code-name Miss Hush was the dancer Martha Graham. The first clue was an allusion to Santa Clause's reindeer, Dancer.

Mama introduced dance as punishment during her time of madness, "Dance, dance, dance" she screamed as she switched at my legs with a belt. My mother introduced dance as unwanted and secret ballet lessons as well as her humiliating demand "Twirl for me." Natalia scared me when she picked me up and like a dervish spun around so I thought I would hurl out of her arms. How could it be that something that began with such pain and fright could be the very thing I now longed for? For all of Rachel's pain and wild movement, she was in control. She had skill. She was in charge. For all her sadness she had a quality about her I could never have named at the time, but now I see her as self-possessed. I did not want to be at the mercy of other people's lives. I believe that the encounter with Rachel was the second hint that it seemed possible to feel in charge of myself. Running through The Sheep Meadow in my own way at my own speed was the first hint.

Perhaps I was able to respond to Rachel so powerfully because while I hated the sports and routines, the camp provided a backdrop of calm and predictability that was in such contrast to life at home. It gave me the emotional space to turn inward without fearing that my sadness, fear, and fury would be unbearable to someone else.

When I returned from camp, Irv had moved out and back to "The Dixie."

My mother was despondent. At one point she even said, "Let's turn on the gas and die." It is hard to believe she actually said that we should turn on the gas and die together. Why did she want me to die with her? She left me many times before to go on with her own life without me. But in death did she want or expect me to go with her? I didn't want to die even if she did. But I also desperately didn't want her to die. I had learned how to say "NO!" around the "Twirl for me." episode and I didn't hold back with this. "NO!" I yelled, "You can't die. I want to live, and I need you to live with me." I was scared by how horribly sad she was and scared at how embarrassed I was that now her second marriage failed. When friends at school asked me where Irv was, I told them he was in China on a business trip, a long business trip. I don't remember how I thought I could keep the lie going.

But why did my mother choose to marry this weirdo from the Hotel Dixie? Certainly, Mama pushed for it. Why did she need to get married at that point? Maybe Sean's requests for children and that she become Catholic were more than she could tolerate, but she could have gone on dating and meet someone else. She was always able to attract men. To her dying days, she attracted men even in her final nursing home. I doubt my wish for a normal family had anything to do with it. I was about to turn ten years old when she decided to marry Irv. She was ten years old when her father deserted her. And soon after he left was when her apartment building caught fire and when the fireman picked her up and threw her down a flight of stairs into the arms of another fireman who waited below and caught her. Was Irv, with his proposal at that moment, the imagined fireman at the bottom of the stairs?

Years later I learned my mother first met Irv soon after she left John. She was his secretary for a while. He loaned her the money to pay for her divorce from John. When she later tried to pay him back, he refused to accept it. Instead, he said to her, "We'll be friends and see each other from time to time." I can imagine, the inflection of his voice rising, "So you'll owe me a favor."

Mosaic

When Irv moved out of the apartment, around 1951, my mother moved into the one bedroom sharing it with me. I was glad to have her close. I was glad we were alone together now, and I was relieved that she decided we would not return to live with Mama.

I couldn't yet face my disappointment in her choice of Irv as a husband and her rejection of Sean. I could no longer idealize her the way I did as a younger child. But now as a young teen, I still needed her. I needed the illusion that she was my home, my protection, and my safe place. Soon her fine porcelain façade would loudly crack for me—but not yet. In some ways, I needed her more than ever. I needed to feel I had a mother before I could leave her. Sometimes she really came through.

She was shaken by her disastrous marriage and its ending, but she managed to find a secretarial job again and her sad mood slowly lifted. After a Mexican divorce from Irv she and I and stayed put in one place for my twelfth, thirteenth and fourteenth years. However, neither she nor I recognized that I too was reacting to her benighted marriage. Somehow we colluded with the notion that it was her business and not mine. Maybe I was willing to go along with this because it took me off the hook of wondering if things might have gone better if I had stayed with Mama instead of moving in with them. Neither of us understood my frequent tearfulness, my continuing poor school performance, and my persistent insomnia. I could not fall asleep until utter exhaustion took over. Why wasn't I happy? I finally had my mother? And ironically the first two years of this period turned out to be our best years together. She did not try to find a new man right away and turned her focus toward me. We were companionable, "Like a Bridge Over Troubled Waters" for one another. Companionable, meaning she wanted my company, but depending on the situation she wanted my company in very different ways at different times. She was a mosaic of different selves. Some were fun, some caring and some selfish.

My mother could be like a supportive older sister who knew something about the world and was helpful as I moved into my more independent teens. And also at times, she could be maternal. Unlike Mama, my mother encouraged me to have friends. She prepared me for getting my period and was willing to answer questions about sex. She attended school functions and became friendly with some of my friend's parents. It was during this time that I started to study dance at the Martha Graham school, and my mother supported it.

She recognized how lost I was at school and negotiated a full scholarship at a local private school with small classes. My grades, however, did not improve until I was in high school.

The interested older sister aspect came out as we spent weekends taking many very long walks through New York, stopping for a pastrami sandwich at Katz's deli or a butterscotch Sundae at Schrafft's or a bag of hot chestnuts from a street vendor. And she talked to me. She spoke about her years growing up, about John's life as an actor with the WPA—

making him seem glamorous. She spoke angrily about Irv, not much about Sean. She talked about the people she met at work.

We were friendly roommates too—sharing the housekeeping, grocery shopping, and even the cooking. I liked to watch one of the first cooking shows on television, The Dione Lucas cooking show. I took pride in being able to make a meal for my mother and me.

However, as she began to date men again, she seemed to forget that I was her daughter and still a young teenager. A new infatuation, even if short-lived, propelled her away from motherhood, back into distracted girlhood. She lost her connection to being a parent and leaned on me as a confident, telling me far too much about her sexual encounters, including with her co-workers and in one instance with the husband of her friend. It was confusing, disturbing and also fascinating. I hated hearing about it yet drawn to learning the mysteries of sex. But I suspect mostly I did not want to lose contact with her and when she was excited or upset about a man. Listening to her was the way to still be with her. I knew she could be motherly and I yearned for it but it was like the words in the love song, "…a sometime thing."

In sharp contrast to her own sexual activity, she was very clear that I should avoid anything sexual. I was not to permit any boy to touch me "above or below." She did not have to worry. I was so frightened to explore sex that it would not be until well into my college years that I allowed myself any adventure. And only when I fell in love with Harry did I allow all the armor to come off.

I did not know how angry I was with her. I did know I was embarrassed by my twice broken home. Nevertheless, her new more sustained interest in me, whether in a motherly or sisterly role or as her confidant meant a lot. I knew she was capable of giving me what I yearned for and I was willing to wait for it.

On one of our very long walks, we passed the Lighthouse for the Blind in mid-town. Suddenly a very frail and old blind woman fell backward onto the sidewalk. My mother knelt beside her and speaking in soothing tones called her "Mother." "Mother, you have fallen. We are going to get you some help right away." Someone ran into The Lighthouse House and called an ambulance. My mother's gentle kindness toward this frightened and probably injured elderly woman still moves me, and I was taken by her calling her "Mother." It certainly bestowed respect, but it also stirred a longing in me. I wanted my mother just to be my mother.

In seventh grade, I was sent to the school psychologist who had an office in a large windowless closet. She grilled me for an hour. I suspect she knew, or at least suspected the marriage to Irv was over. She didn't say this but kept asking what we did together as a family. "Did the three of us have dinner together?" "Did we do things together on weekends?" "Oh yes, we did." I lied, sweating and shaking. I would not confess that my mother messed up again or that my living with them may have caused the marriage to fail, or that I was telling my classmates that Irv (or "my father" as I falsely referred to him) was in China. She asked how I felt about school. I told her I hated fractions because I could not understand them. But as for her questions about family life, I lied to that psychologist to end of the hour. She finally let me leave. I trembled as I walked back to the classroom; then breathed again saying to myself, "You protected Mommy." I was, of course, protecting myself from my fury and very nervous about being caught in a web of my own lies.

From age twelve on, I slowly made the transition from calling my mother Mommy to calling her Marion. She preferred it, and I suspect it helped me to come to grips, if not to terms with her failure to create a marriage for herself and a family with two functioning parents for me.

166

However, the good aspects of our companionable time together made a real difference for me. I appreciated her resilience, her ability to enjoy things, her artistic flair, and her ability to get people interested in her. And she supported my urgent need to dance.

Marion Comes Through—
Walking the Rhythm

During these years, Marion and I often went to an off-off-Broadway Theater in the South Village. I don't remember exactly where it was located. Perhaps it was on Bleecker Street or Lafayette Street. I also don't remember the name of the theatre, but I will call it "The Theatre of Blue Shadows." We lived close by so we had only to walk a short distance to see the plays. Housed in a five-story tenement walk-up the "theater" had no stage, only a portion of space marked off with room for about twenty folding chairs. The curtain was a clothesline hung with rags. No tickets were needed. A donation basket passed at intermission. The new plays were raw, unedited, still wet with ink. It was a place of opportunity for young wannabe actors, washed-up actors, and new or old unpublished playwrights. The harvest of their unpaid efforts was to be visible, to be discovered or re-discovered. The company considered itself experimental and improvisational. I loved going there. It was part of my newly blooming artistic, bohemian, New York identity.

Occasionally the group rented the space to other performers. I frequently checked the Village Voice to see what was playing. Because

168

I was still too young to make the night trip alone, Marion was a good sport and took me to performances. She also seemed to enjoy it. She had been a wannabe actor herself, so perhaps she relished feeling nostalgic for that period of her life. Did she hope John might show up in such a place? Did I?

This particular time when I checked the "Voice" I saw that a visiting troupe of African dancers and drummers were going to perform on Friday, Saturday and Sunday night. I was thrilled. I was having a distant love affair with Africa. It all began with the exotic photographs published in National Geographic magazine followed by many trips to the African exhibits at the Museum of Natural History. Then my fascination was fully inflamed with the movie "King Solomon's Mines" starring Deborah Kerr and Stewart Granger. The Watusi dancers and the battle of the Watusi kings especially captured me.

Decades later I recall imploring Harry to drive twenty miles to a distant town to see a single showing of the movie. Later I saw that it was to play on the "Late Show" on television but we did not own a television and so we went to the local Laundromat where there was a TV. We did our laundry and watched the movie at 11pm. Except for the Watusi dancers, the rest of the movie now seemed colonial and sentimental.

So going back to the early 1950's; on Friday night Marion and I walked to the South Village and climbed the five flights of stairs. Out came the troupe of men and women dancers and all male drummers and singers—perhaps as many performers as there were people in the audience. They were dressed in brief skirts and loincloths. The women, although not bare-breasted, wore minimal coverings. The drummers began, and soon the dancers joined in. The passionate, percussive sounds and movement shook the old building. The dancers' brawny bodies of pure muscle and rhythm pounded the stage with their feet and in counter rhythm thrust and swayed their pelvises, heads, and limbs. The singers joined in with exotic clicks and vibrant words full of first hard then soft sounds.

The vibrations entered my chest, then spread. No longer a singular person watching a performance, I seemed to disperse becoming the drums, the dancers, the voices, the spectacle, the beat. When they ended, the audience erupted with applause shouting "bravo." Slowly I collected myself. Still transfixed, we walked home. Saturday came, and I could not stop thinking of the African dancers and musicians. I asked Marion if we could go again on Saturday night. She paused, sighed, and said, "OK—I guess we can." Off we went, and I had the same experience all over again. Then Sunday arrived. I wanted to go again. I couldn't stand the thought of the group doing a final performance and me missing it. I waited until late afternoon and asked again if we could go. Marion's first words were, "It's a school night. You can't stay up late on a school night. And I have to be at work tomorrow as well." I backed off until after dinner, and then I begged. "The group is returning to Africa—we might never see a live group of African dancers again. This is our chance of a lifetime!" She rolled her eyes and gave in. Off we went again, and it was as wonderful as the two nights before.

Now I wonder why she was willing to do that. Three nights in a row she walked to the South Village, climbed five flights of smelly, rickety stairs in a firetrap building because I begged her to. I think she enjoyed it the first time, but it was not her thing. Why did she do it?

She was still recovering from her divorce from Irv. I suspect we clung to each other in states of shared regret and sadness. There was a history to that. I heard that when I was still a baby before she left John, they fought bitterly through the night. She told me that to get out of the fray, she would pick me up from my crib and leave the apartment. Carrying me, she walked the streets of Upper-Broadway where we lived. When I imagine those night walks, the rhythm of her step as she ascended and descended the hilly sidewalks holding me against her body, I can imagine the beating of her heart and mine, the warmth, the melancholy and the closeness. Perhaps that is why I so wanted to walk with my mother and feel the beat and rhythm of the African dancers, as I had once felt the rhythm and beat of being close to her. Perhaps she too felt it, and maybe that is why she was willing to go to that performance three times.

My Brilliant Shopper

Marion was a brilliant shopper. She worked in mid-town Manhattan. During her lunch hours, she went to only the best stores, Bonwit Teller, Saks 5th Avenue, Lord &Taylor, and Batman. She never bought a thing. What she did do was to scope out the styles, the brand names, the textiles, and fashionable colors. She made a point of reading fashion magazines. After she divorced Irv, she changed her style of dressing to something more relaxed and youthful again. No more Chanel suits, but a different style with more flow. I would call it Glamour Magazine, New York working girl, ingénue. She was petite and pretty and looked younger than her age. She took full advantage of it.

She went on a shopping spree twice a year. She picked me up after her workday, and we walked from our downtown apartment to S. Klein's at Union Square and 14th Street. Klein's was a deep discount women's department store. It was a big warehouse with fluorescent lights and a linoleum floor. As you walked in you smelled the preservatives and chemicals of cheap clothes. There were some regular clothes racks, but most of the clothes were thrown into huge wooden bins separated by size and garment—skirts in one, sweaters in another, blouses, scarves, handbags, jackets and some children's clothes as well. The secret of Klein's that every woman knew was that hidden amongst the junk were treasures—the very treasures that Marion had already eyed in the best stores. They ended up at Klein's because they were left over from last season, they were "seconds" or models had already worn them in fashion shows. Everything, the junk and the treasures, landed higgledy-piggledy together into the bins. On arrival at Klein's, we joined the feeding frenzy of female humanity pushing their way to the front of the bins. If it was the size ten sweater bin, there was everything from Orlon to cashmere, from fuchsia and bilious chartreuse to subtle earth tones and delicate pastels—but the junk was always in ascendance. The trick was to get up to the bin, eye the chaotic pile, reach in and pull out something from the mess that looked promising. You had to be aggressive. You had to have learned the pushing technique from the subway rush hours. Marion was brilliant at this, not only because she had a perfect eye for what she could have easily found on a quiet rack at Saks, but also she had trained her eye for what the good stuff looked like even when it was buried in junk. And most importantly she was quick and shifty, dodging under and around the women already at the front of the bin. Then when she saw a fragment of what might be a treasure, she dove with the swiftness of a kingfisher, grabbed the garment and flung it to my waiting arms while I stood a yard or so behind the stampeding crowd.

Marion was unique. I never saw her get into one of the many fights between women pulling at the same garment. If one of them didn't yield the garment could rip. Or the contretemps could deteriorate into some pummeling. Klein's was not for sissies. You had to be either tough or very quick. Marion was quick. I always felt proud of her skill.

When finished with the bins we needed to sort and so sought out a small open space where we would not be trampled. There were no try-on rooms. You tried on things over your street clothes. You dressed light for

Klein's. You also might pull up a skirt under the skirt you were already wearing. We made our choices, flung what we didn't want back into the bins and took our loot to the cashier. Then came the best part. Our athletic shopping worked up our appetites, so next, we went to Klein's basement cafeteria. The décor was pale blue Formica counters, chrome stools, more linoleum, and more fluorescent light. Décor aside, Klein's was ahead of its time. It was the only eating establishment that served bagels, long before bagels moved uptown and became ecumenical. Not only did they have bagels, but also Klein's kitchen was the first to invent the pizza bagel—with a little smear of tomato sauce and some Kraft American cheese. A warm pizza bagel, gooey, crunchy and savory with a forbidden coke was a just reward for our efforts.

Then began our triumphant march homeward. Every once in a while I slipped my hand into the shopping bag to feel the glorious silk, the soft cashmere, and the smooth leather.

As the years passed and I became an older teenager, in opposition to Marion's style, I defined my own—New York, bohemian, artistic. I devoted my wardrobe to the black turtleneck and long paisley skirt. But I always accompanied her to Klein's to catch the flying garments and to enjoy the pizza bagels and the forbidden coke.

During this period I believe I saw the best of Marion. Watching her at the Klein's bins, as humorous as that was it was also a moment when I saw her competence. Her competence was clearly there, but she never fully developed it. She was smart but didn't allow herself to seek an education. She was a hostage to her need to be taken care of by a man. Was she stuck as the abandoned ten-year-old daughter, whose father left her, never to return and never to contact her? We know he lived because when he died Mama was in her sixties and heard from a distant relative about his death. Marion was in her forties, and she had heard nothing from him for over thirty years.

Good Times/Bad Times

The memory of Rachel's powerful dance performance at summer camp and our conversation about her training stayed with me. I thought about it long after. It became an oasis I wanted to find. When I turned thirteen, I often walked home from school slowly, stopping to browse in the many neighborhood second-hand bookstores on lower Broadway. I liked old Life Magazines and books of photographs. One afternoon I was excited to come upon a book of remarkable dance photographs of Martha Graham and her company. The photographer, Barbara Morgan caught on camera the vibrant dance movements that so roused me when Rachel gave her performance. I asked Marion if she would go to the bookstore and buy the book. She did. It cost ten dollars. It remains a treasure.

Later, on a walk through the area near Washington Square Park on lower Fifth Avenue, I came upon a sign for the Martha Graham School. I asked Marion if I could take classes there and she agreed and again negotiated a scholarship.

Soon, every Saturday morning I walked alone from our apartment on Waverly Place to the Martha Graham School and took the children's classes with Erick Hawkins, a sensitive and skilled teacher, but most importantly he became an advocate and mentor and also forged a tie

175

with Marion. It wasn't a romantic tie. It was as though he included her in my education as a dancer often suggesting concerts or exhibits she might take me to. I have no idea whether he intuited that to be a mentor to me he would need to attend to Marion as well, but he understood something about us that worked very well and set me on the right path. He became a model for a man I might fall in love with someday—kind, generous and smart. If Marion tried to flirt with him, he responded with grace, neither falling for it nor rejecting her.

The experience of dance with Erick was so profoundly different from the secret ballet classes. I wanted this, I asked for it. It was a first step of feeling something was my own. I was also wresting my body away from Mama, Marion, and Natalia. It felt like the very beginning of taking charge of myself, but just the beginning.

Then, like Rachel, I too went on to study dance at the High School of Performing Arts.

My freshman year at Performing Arts was very difficult. I had less training than some of the other students and was far behind them. Also, I had my period for the first time. I felt sad about it. My body was getting ahead of me. I wanted more time as a child. But I threw myself into training this strange new body, taking additional technique classes on weekends and holidays.

Also during sophomore year, on friendly terms, I left Erick Hawkins' Studio. He, like me, was entering a new phase of his life. It did not escape me that he was falling in love with Hanna, a thirty-year-old woman in his dance company. Also, by this time he broke away from Martha Graham's technique and was developing his own unique style. I, on the other hand, redoubled my efforts to develop greater skill in the Graham technique.

I always loved to jump and leap, but now I was learning to move with precision. A leaping dancer sometimes appears suspended in air.

A slight shift of movement at the apex of the leap gives this illusion. Leaping is a remarkable movement of strength, control, and defiance, defiance of gravity.

With more technique and skill, I found ways to express and inform myself about my sadness and anger as I had seen in Rachel's dance, but I also experienced soaring joy, even ecstasy feeling the power of my increasing physical strength and flexibility.

I loved lifts with a dance partner. They are thrilling. The shared movements rely on the dependency, trust, and autonomy of both partners. While it looks like the lifter does most of the work, it is equally divided using mutual counter-weight, coordinated breath, and timing. Lifts are a metaphor for both accommodation and independence with another person. They are about working out a relationship.

I was also getting more involved in the activities of my own life. I regularly used New York public transportation. Even late at night, there was always a crowd of people. I came and went to rehearsals, classes, and concerts often arriving home in time to go to bed.

Eventually, Marion began to date again, urgently. Having emerged from the flames of her second divorce, she began to fly into the waiting arms of a few different men.

She had no difficulty attracting men. She met them at work, or through friends, or at a cocktail lounge, she and her co-workers frequented after work. Briefly, she dated the divorced father of a friend of mine. My friend and I giddily imagined being sisters. Our high hopes were soon dashed. Marion dropped him. Maybe he, like Sean, was too interested in being a family.

She began to see married men. Perhaps there were fewer available single men. Maybe it wasn't new. My father, although possibly struggling with being gay, was married when they began to spend time together

She wanted closeness with me, but more and more she wanted me as her confidant. I was frightened by her stories of the men who found her irresistible. There was something predatory in how she described the men she met and how they pursued her. There was also something predatory in her urge to tell me about it.

When Marion was between men or the married men were off with their families, she was particularly needy and depended on my company.

One evening after dinner we lingered over the teacups, and Marion suddenly said, "You know Phil, my friend Emily's husband. He gave me a lift to work. He said he loved my perfume. Then I saw he had an erection. He asked me to touch it." She paused. I did not want to hear more. I wanted to run but felt nailed to the seat. Gathering up all the false sophistication I could muster I asked, "So what did you do?" Staring into her dreamy middle distance with eyelids at half-mast she answered, "I helped him calm down."

How can you tell your daughter something like that? Why did I tolerate it? I ask this now. Why couldn't I get up from the table at that point yelling, "Shut up, I don't want to hear your stories about sex with your men, especially not the husband of your friend or any married man, or maybe any man." I couldn't say it. Why? Was the sex fascinating even though it scared me? Why did she need to tell me about her conquests? Was she trying to show me how to attract men? Was she competing with me? Was she the queen/witch from Snow White? "Mirror, mirror on the wall, who is the fairest of us all?" She was in her early forties. She said she feared to lose her good looks. Her worries were unfounded. In her early nineties, she still turned the heads of octogenarians.

I put on an act of worldliness and acceptance with her but with friends, when they far more fittingly than my mother spoke about their sexual adventures I withdrew from them and ended the friendship. I still needed her. In spite of my slowly emerging independence, I feared if I didn't have her, I would have no one. She was my mother. Who else was there? Was I so desperate for her attention that I settled for what I could get from her? Did I need her the way she needed her men?

Breakfast at Walgreens

Early in my junior year, Marion wanted a fresh start and she was able to find a new apartment in New York City's Stuyvesant Town. On the morning after our big move, she said there was nothing to eat in the apartment. I should leave extra early to stop for breakfast at the Walgreens soda fountain on Broadway, right near the high school. I agreed and took an earlier subway. As I sat down at the counter, I was dazed by the choices on the menu. I had never eaten breakfast alone in a restaurant. What possibly could I choose to eat? I took the most familiar thing I could find, Rice Krispies. As I spooned it up, I heard the familiar, comforting sounds of "Snap, Crackle, and Pop."

I left Walgreens to walk the few blocks through the theatre district to school. I suddenly felt excited, free, and even triumphant. Why did I wonder? It felt new.

Many of the girls in my class seemed very sophisticated to me. They had , and some were exploring sex. It all scared me. Working hard and gaining more dance technique seemed like a counterbalance to all the heady sexuality. Any sexual yearnings I experienced only made me dance all the harder.

By late sophomore year, I caught up with my class and also was invited to dance in some group dances choreographed by senior students. I began to feel hopeful and capable as a dancer.

That morning, after Walgreens, I walked the rest of the way to school. I thought there is a real chance I can become a working dancer, maybe even a choreographer. I can take care of myself—after all, I just got my own breakfast at Walgreens. When I think back to that important moment, I know that for the first time a new thought slowly emerged; I could shape my future. I couldn't control it completely and could change nothing in the past, but now more than ever before I had a future that could include what I wanted. I could create my life, how I lived it and the people I chose to be in it. I had already found Rachel and Erick and knowing them changed me. I began to understand what it meant to be self—possessed, although I still had a long way to go before I felt it. Rachel and Erick were my first models.

I wanted exciting and meaningful work. I wanted to continue to meet interesting and creative people. In spite of my present fears, I also wanted to fall in love and make a normal family. That wasn't a new thought, but that morning for the first time it seemed possible. I was not fated to live a life like the women who raised me.

This was the time when Marc, my second imaginary companion, the competent, problem solving, good sport, strong and wiry boy, shifted from being a secret invisible companion living in my pocket to a more internal part of me. Making my inner companion male was also a counter-force to what I saw as Marion's hyper-femininity and neediness that seemed to get her into so much trouble. I began to think she too readily gave over her body and her voice to others. She chose and succumbed to a variety of men who wanted to control her like a child. She could, at least temporarily, melt into the mold she thought they wanted or needed her to be until she could no longer tolerate their demands and then moved onto the next man who turned her head with his flattery. Sadly, she remained convinced her feminine beauty was her only coin of the realm. Did she ever trust or enjoy her own company?

I wanted to defy that kind of passivity and control by others, yet I still wanted to love someone. I began to search for new role models, women who lived full lives with compelling work, with partners and children. They were not likely to be dancers, but I had yet to learn that. But dance did give me control of my body and some confidence. It was the first step.

By the time I was sixteen, I did belong more to myself than to Marion, Mama, and Natalia but it took a long time before I could let anyone else be close.

As a small child, I was shrouded with fear that my mother would die and I would either be sent away or be trapped with my grandmother. To feel safe, I relied on the magic of numbers and ritual. As a teenager, I still relied on magic and ritual, but I also began to cope with the family chaos by seeking my own order, structure, and discipline, probably to an extreme. On weekends, I did homework, attended additional dance classes and went to rehearsals. It was orderly but not altogether austere. On Saturday nights I went folk dancing. I met a few young men while folk dancing, even went on a few dates but nothing developed and I probably saw to it that it didn't. When I had the time, I listened to music, went alone to museums, dance concerts, and for long walks through the city watching people, acquainting myself with neighborhoods and enjoying the movement, the freedom and rhythm of the walk. On my long walks, I sometimes wondered if I passed John. By then I had not seen or heard from him for about twelve years, but he was rarely far from my mind. If I passed him, would I know him? Would he know me? I doubted it.

I had a few friends among my fellow dancers but I didn't vigorously pursue and nourish relationships. I had moments of feeling lonely, especially when I saw some girls in my class regularly hanging out in a coffee shop near school, smoking and laughing together. I was invited to a couple of sweet sixteen parties and saw what seemed like social ease amongst the teenagers. I felt like an outsider but I was also filled with the thrill of being a dancer and with my ambition to join a major dance company and perform.

Words into Dance /
Dance into Words

Around the time of starting high school, I saw one of Martha Graham's last performances. At her advanced age, her physical skill was waning, but her sense of drama was as profound as ever. She performed "Letter to The World" based on the poems of Emily Dickinson. The music of Hunter Johnson, the spoken words of Dickinson's poems and Graham's inventive movement, all beautifully performed, seamlessly wove together. Deeply stirred by both the dance and the words, seeing "Letter to the World" became another pivotal moment in my life, similar to what I felt at the time of Rachel, the dance counselor's, performance. The passionate entwining of words and dance in "Letter to the World", struck me with a force I had not fully realized before. I was a reader and loved stories and drama, but I had not imagined that I too could find words to express strong feelings. I wanted both dance and words and became especially drawn to dance teachers and choreographers who were also verbally eloquent. Through richly expressive language as well as dance they taught their students and company dancers nuances of feeling and meanings of movement. I was fascinated by the power of their words to elicit emotion and actually change how the dancers moved.

During the summer before senior year, I worked as a demonstrator for a former principal member of the Martha Graham Company, Jane Dudley. She was in her late forties, and advancing arthritis brought an end to her performing life. This was not an unusual situation. A dancer's life is short. It ends when other careers are ripening into maturity.

Jane Dudley was still a sought after teacher. That summer she had a contract to teach an adult class in New Jersey. Each week we met at the Port Authority Bus Depot and spent an hour each way on the bus, talking. On those rides, precious to me, she mused freely about her art and her life. She appeared to accept that her performing career was over, but her intelligence and poetic language inspired both her students and me.

"Letter to the World" and eloquent dancers illuminated the connection between movement, feeling, and language which then brought me to poetry, literature, psychology and a search to voice the ineffable which eventually led to becoming a psychoanalyst.

At the end of junior year, I joined a dance company, first as an understudy and then senior year performed with the company. I also had other opportunities to perform. Dance offered much of what I hoped for and carried me safely through my teen years. I continued to find thoughtful, and stimulating people, like Jane Dudley.

When John hung me upside down, when Natalia frantically swirled me around the room, when Mama confined me to the house, when I was lifted into the washtubs at The Green Grass School, I had no control and no voice. Dance and certain dancers taught me that I could take control of my body and my voice and possibly take control of my life.

The Present Reveals the Past

Just before entering college in 1956, the dancer and choreographer Pearl Lang created a dance/drama, using both words and dance movement for a television program. I had a principal role. My co-dancers, Robert Cohan, Bertram Ross, and Paul Taylor were all at that time seasoned performers in Martha Graham's Company. There was also an experienced woman dancer, Anita Denks who was in Merce Cunningham's company. I had seen all of them perform many times before.

Rehearsing and performing with this small group of established dancers gave me a valuable chance to have some real sense of a professional dancer's daily life. They were fiercely disciplined, maintaining their physical skills with daily classes and endless rehearsals. Their body was their Stradivarius. They were highly intelligent. They also shaped their lives to the demands of the choreographer. Rehearsals were scheduled anytime and could last as long as the choreographer wanted to work. The dancer's weight, especially the woman dancer's weight, was constantly scrutinized by the choreographer. Anorexia is rampant among dancers. Few dancers can maintain a desirable weight without deprivation that verges on starvation. Because the television camera tended to make bodies look bigger, I was told to lose ten pounds before the filming.

Dancers often went on tour with their companies for long or short periods and were expected to disconnect from their home lives whenever a tour could be arranged. And if they were injured, not uncommon, they either danced with their injuries and through their pain or were out, sometimes for a while and sometimes permanently.

The familiar unpredictability of the working dancer's life mirrored my childhood. Where would I be tomorrow? Where would I be next year? Dance, so far, had brought me freedom and independence, especially from my family, but a professional dancer who was not, or not yet, a

186

choreographer gave over his or her body and life to the choreographer and to the company. Was the thrill of dancing and performing enough? It became a compelling question. Was there anything else that could bring the satisfaction that dance brought?

Ultimately I turned away from the life of a dancer. It was not only the concerns raised here but also some experiences I could not tolerate. Some choreographers could be sadistic and humiliating. Once in a final rehearsal on stage with some people watching in the audience, the choreographer became frustrated with a new young dancer who at the time was wearing a red leotard. "Get your fat, red behind off this stage!" he screamed. The dancer fled. Then a few minutes later the choreographer screamed again, "Now get back here!" and the tear-streaked young woman obeyed. It was horrifying to watch.

My own humiliation occurred while rehearsing a piece where I had a leading part. The choreographer decided I should be "wilder" in a certain section and told my male partner to hit me, not as part of the dance itself but I think to rile me up. I was outraged. Yet, like the poor dancer clad in red, I too did not yell, "Stop it!" I couldn't shake the experience. It was the last time I danced in a professional company. I had reached a point when the captivity, the scrutiny, the potential to be badly treated and humiliated was too much of a repetition of what I had already lived through. It brought back Marion's demand that I twirl for her and Mama screaming "dance!" while hitting me with a belt. Working as a professional dancer seemed to hold too many eerie new editions of those old events. As a child, I could not escape. As a teenager, the years of dance training gave me a taste of freedom, most importantly freedom from the women who raised me. But I came to realize the life of a professional dancer was not an escape, not a freedom run. Did I want a professional life that was so demanding, even cruel and tyrannical at times? It was a life that left little time and energy for love and the extraordinary, ordinary life I so much wanted. I would not have been content only to be a dancer in the corps. A principal dancer faced even more demands. Unless you were a choreographer, and at that point, I had no idea if I had the interest or talent for it, dance could be a form of slavery under the choreographer's control.

College years—A New Direction

I left the dance company and began college. I continued to dance in college for three of the four years but no longer felt the same commitment to it. Taking dance classes, performing in college recitals and teaching children's classes in the community was a placeholder just in case I returned to it; or maybe a life raft until I found solid ground again. I majored in literature and psychology.

Junior year in college I tried to integrate my developing interests by writing a paper on using verbal imagery and metaphor to teach dance, but more importantly, I took a developmental psychology course with an inspiring teacher, Marianne Lester. Professor Lester was also a clinician working with young children in psychotherapy. In some ways, she reminded me of Rachel from camp. Rachel expressed powerful feeling through movement. Professor Lester expressed powerful feelings through straightforward talk. She spoke movingly about her work with young, troubled children helping them to give voice to worries about themselves and their families. I often wished, that as a child, someone had brought me to see her. I also began to think that not only could I benefit from psychotherapy and psychoanalysis; it also might be a direction to pursue as a career. I also took note that Professor Lester had a family life with a husband and two children.

In her course, we read Freud and some of his followers including Erik Erikson. Some of their writings vividly describe how the child's mind develops out of his or her early experiences of the body. Along with the innate constitution, how the caretaker handles and tends to the child's body shapes how the child will think about him or herself. Experiences of pain, pleasure, comfort, satisfaction and the freedom to move all play their part. Sensitivity to the child's rhythms of movement and needs have a major role in forming the developing person's trust in others. How the caretaker speaks to the child and helps him or her to be a part of the world all contribute to determining who the child will be. The body and mind are mutually dynamic and entwined. The body for as long as it is alive is always in motion, and so is the mind. The body continuously pulses, moves and breathes and the mind constantly perceives, sorts, integrates, fragments, re-constitutes, seeks, hides, reveals. Also, minds and bodies are hardwired to move and to engage with other minds and bodies.

Much later, when I pursued studies to become a psychoanalyst, for sure the personal psychoanalysis was the most crucial part of the training. The most memorable course I took was a child psychoanalysis seminar given weekly at 7:30 a.m. Four male child psychoanalysts spoke about their work with small children and the children's parents. I continued to attend that 7:30 a.m. seminar long after it was required and long after I was a practicing psychoanalyst until most of those psychoanalysts retired. I was well aware that it was not only the content of what they talked about and its relevance to my work with adults that compelled me to go. I also wanted to listen to grown men who were interested in the worries of little children and liked to talk to them.

The shift from dance to healing troubled minds had, of course, much to do with the wish to continue healing myself and also with my longing to engage with others through what I have come to call real talk. Real talk, with anyone, with patients, friends, or family is as stripped of pretense, illusion, and self-protectiveness as is possible although never perfect. It is talk that invites another to also engage in real talk. Real talk need not be concrete or simple. It has layers of meaning expressed by metaphor, tone, rhythm, and timing that gives it its power and its realness.

When I think of real talk with a patient it is when we have had an exchange that for the moment feels full of relevant meaning and the patient has discovered a new thought or considers an old thought in a new way. After such a moment there is usually silence when we both take a breath—a moment of taking what we have learned into our bodies as well as our minds.

When I think of real talk in ordinary conversation, I think of Natalia telling me that John was gay. It helped me enormously to begin to feel sympathy for his unbearable situation during his lifetime. Again Natalia, by telling me she knew she was dying allowed me to feel close to her, even when she was also raging and psychotic. I still wonder if she was my biological mother—not impossible. It again invites that question, who was my father? Is that why John never called or wrote? I will never have an answer, but the questions are real talk and give shape to the Pote/pot, although briefly. As long as I am alive in body and mind, the Pote/pot remains in a constant motion of shapeshifting.

As a six-year-old, filled with my physical power, I ran across Sheep Meadow, zigzagging, spinning, backward and forward toward and away from my mother, heady with the bodily joy of it. The path from Sheep Meadow was tortuous but winds forward to Rachel, to my eloquent dance teachers and choreographers, to studying psychology, to literature, to psychoanalysis and a life long search to find words for the ineffable. It also traced a future path for falling in love.

Part IV

DAMAGE AND REPAIR

The Porcelain Shatters— Marion's Men and Mine

Marion's Men

Marion continued to date married men hoping someone would leave his wife to be with her.

When I began college, she began an affair with Walter. Walter was married and had teenage children. He told Marion he would divorce his wife, but he frequently spent time with his family. As far as I know, Marion was faithful to him, waited for the divorce to happen (it didn't) and willing to be alone when he was busy. I didn't know why.

Walter was a corporate executive. He was a big man with white hair and a puffy red face. He dressed in dark three-piece suits and expensive silk ties.

Marion told me they met one rainy day at a taxi stand near the apartment building. She said he stepped up to protect her with his man-size umbrella and then offered to share his cab with her. He lived nearby in one of the more elegant New York buildings.

When I came home from college for weekends or holidays, Walter was often at the apartment. He and I shared no common ground. We had little to say to each other, but we remained stiffly cordial.

He and Marion didn't appear to talk much either. They played a lot of gin rummy and drank. He drank a lot, sometimes turning maudlin and pathetic reaching out for Marion and telling her how much he loved her. Marion tolerated this. She claimed his drinking did not interfere with his work. She told me she would marry him if he were free, but he made no move to divorce or even separate from his wife.

The affair seemed to be secret yet not secret. He invited Marion to his Club for elaborate lunches. If I was at home, they sometimes invited me to come along. For reasons I don't understand I often joined them. I said little and felt awkward being there. Here I was out with Marion and her stuffy, at least slightly drunk, married lover, sitting in a rich man's corporate "club" where I gluttonously ate the fancy food until I felt I would burst; my bloated stomach serving as a soporific cushion. I could not see what she saw in him but she readily made herself available to him when he was free to see her. He had a powerful influence on her. Suddenly she became a Republican. I had decided this was all her business until I felt how her transformation also affected me.

I had become friendly with a choreographer, a former teacher of mine, and his wife who was also a dancer. They were about ten years older and somewhere between mentors and friends. When I was in the City, I visited them at their apartment and also invited them to Marion's apartment as well. I had the impression that she enjoyed them too. We shared meals and conversations and Marion was always included when they came over. The man was black and the woman white. Suddenly Marion announced that I could no longer invite them home. She was vague at first about why and when I pressed her she said Walter thought it was a bad idea for other people in the building to see that we entertained a "colored" man. I objected, of course, saying she had not had any misgivings before, why suddenly now? She protested saying Walter had convinced her. I was furious, but also it dawned on me that one way to understand Marion is that she became like whomever she was with. When Marion was with my father, they readily socialized with the Black actors who were also a part of the W.P.A. And she was willing to dress in men's clothes to go to McSorley's with him. With Irv, she tried on the role of a domestic housewife who enhanced the stature of her husband by being decorative in return for material security. Now, with Walter, she drank more and became a bigot. Woo her and she's yours.

I don't know what Walter's wife or son knew about Marion until one weekend when Marion and I were alone at the apartment the doorbell rang and a young man introduced himself as Walter's son. He was about eighteen. Marion told me to go into the bedroom but I soon heard the son shouting at Marion, and I came out to see him close up to her and screaming in her face. I yelled at him, "Get out or I'll call the police!" and he left. The affair continued and as far as I know, Walter's son stayed out of it.

Once during a holiday break from college, I was home at my desk trying to write a paper when Marion came to the door pleading, "Please talk to me. I'm so lonely. I need you to talk to me." Walter was off with his family. I did not feel sympathetic. By then Natalia, my aunt, had moved in with Mama and except for going to work, Natalia was in Mama's thrall, ensnared in Mama's hypochondria and her tyrannical demand that Natalia always account for her whereabouts. If Natalia was late Mama greeted her in a state of panic and fury, maybe like my panic and fury as a nine-year-old when Marion was late.

At that moment, when Marion came to the door pleading I talk to her, I knew if I became available to her, I could get trapped with my mother like Natalia was trapped with hers. I stopped coming home on weekends and began to spend more time at school. I was glad to have the privacy and the opportunity to concentrate on schoolwork and even socialize more with other students. Even though my actions appeared more independent, my feelings were full of contradictions. I was relieved to be away from Marion, but I also missed her and was homesick especially on weekends when the college emptied. I had my own brand of ensnaring her by feeling so unsure of my ability to write college-level papers that I insisted on reading them to her over the phone to get her help or approval. It made no sense. I was already more educated than she was, but I needed her reassurance, and she was willing to spend the time for reasons I don't understand. What did she get out of it? Maybe she was lonely and wanted my company when Walter wasn't available. Or perhaps she was looking for a vicarious education or felt some satisfaction that I still depended on her or maybe she was able to take some pleasure in being supportive. When I remember it now, I wonder if, for me, it was a way to be close to her with a focused activity at a safe distance, less likely to end up with her telling me about her sex life. If I felt I needed to read something to her, I called, and if she was busy, we made a plan when I could have a long time with her on the phone. This seemed to offer something for each of us, but only briefly.

Later that year I came home one weekend without announcing it first. I opened the door of the apartment with my key and stepped into a small foyer before the entrance into the living room. I heard Marion gasp and cry out, "Who is it?" She and Walter were obviously having sex in the living room out of my sight but well within my hearing. I lingered at the coat closet and chatted away nonsensically while listening to the rustle of clothing being adjusted. Once all seemed in order, I walked in. Soon Walter left, and before the end of the weekend, Marion asked for my apartment key. I, of course, knew she wanted it so that I would not intrude on them again. However, she chose to say that she was afraid I would lose the key and as a woman living alone she feared intruders. I can't imagine that she didn't know that I understood perfectly well why I was to give up my key. Yet I can also imagine that she thought me so naïve that I would buy her story. And yet again I believed I needed to shield her from my anger, so there was no real talk. Caught between still needing her and needing to have little to do with her, I knew this was the end of returning to the apartment as though it was home. I did return to the apartment many times again but always first asking, *Mother may I*. I told myself I was just as glad to not come home without an invitation. I did not want to walk in on a sex scene again. I was angry but mostly hurt and scared.

Even though I looked at Natalia's situation with horror and no way would I ever agree to live with Marion again, the future loomed with uncertainty with no safety net below called home.

I developed a physical symptom. I lost my balance. I continued to take dance classes just in case I wanted to go back to it, but after years of excellent ability to balance easily on one foot, even on tiptoe, I could no longer do it. Also, I occasionally fell when walking. There was nothing physically wrong, so I decided to see the school psychiatrist, a well-known psychoanalyst in his day. He was of no help. He wanted to explore whether I was dating or not. I told him I seemed to be able to meet young men but didn't especially enjoy dating for dating's sake. Did he wonder if I was a Lesbian but could not face it and that is what was throwing me off balance? Did I wonder? I suppose if he and I continued to meet, which we did not, I might have begun talking about how disturbing I found my mother's sexuality, my fury at her and how I still yearned to be her child.

Walter had his wife and family, and he had Marion at his convenience. Did Marion believe Walter was her last chance? When he was not available, I suspect her loneliness was particularly malignant. But I couldn't and didn't want to fix it.

And Mine

Now, in my women's college, surrounded by women falling in and out of love I tentatively began to explore my erotic interests. Not surprisingly, this heralded a series of collisions with Marion that created a rupture we never mended.

By the end of sophomore year, I began to have boyfriends whom I enjoyed. At some point when I liked the person, I was seeing I brought him home to meet Marion. She flirted with all of them. She didn't know how not to flirt.

Once a boyfriend told me he liked my mother so much we should just spend the evening in the apartment with her. That was the end of him.

Then I met Frank whom I liked a lot. He was energetic, enthusiastic and had an animal vitality about him. He smelled great—like clean earth. He was a senior in college, a science major but he was also a violinist and an actor. He was struggling to decide which of his talents to pursue. He was interested that I danced and encouraged me to go back to it professionally. I brought him home to meet Marion. She of course flirted, but Frank was more interested in me. I continued to see him on weekends. We spent time in New York, so he often picked me up at the apartment.

One Saturday, when I returned to the apartment late, Marion first criticized me for holding hands with Frank in front of her. Then, scrutinizing my appearance, I was wearing a form-fitting red dress, she roughly instructed, "You are getting broad in the beam. You better start wearing a girdle if you are going to wear a tight red dress like that." Now in her forties, her body edges had softened. She wore a one-piece-two-way-stretch undergarment that squeezed her into a shape she found more acceptable. I don't think I could have tolerated such confinement of my flesh for more than five minutes. Nevertheless, I bought a small girdle, tried to wear it once then threw it into the back of the closet along with the red dress. She probably thought I looked sexy and that was her domain. Marion's comment was so reminiscent of the poor young woman who was shouted off stage by the choreographer, "Get your fat red behind off this stage." It should have felt eerily similar except for the very real possibility that I had already told her about that horrifying event. It seemed that when it came to men, she and I were engaged in an undeclared war using any hit and run tactics at hand. Soon I would use tactics of my own.

One Sunday Marion visited me at college and as we were walking on the path to lunch she told me angrily that I should stop seeing Frank. "I know the type. He is not for you!" If she had any argument about why Frank wasn't for me I don't remember what it was. However, I had some anxieties of my own about Frank that she did not know about. Frank was pressuring me to have sex, and when I brought up the question of birth control, probably as a delaying tactic more than a plan, he said he trusted withdrawal as a method. I knew that didn't make sense. I suddenly sensed his animal vitality might be like a lion laying claim to a lioness, and then getting her pregnant.

Someone had recently characterized me as "too bloody serious". I agreed. Marion was the one with the sexual charms who attracted men lustily; I just read poetry with my boyfriends and indulged in some carefully controlled foreplay. All I could think of was how terrible it would be to get pregnant. It would be the end of my newly won independent life away from Marion. Marion had flings. I did not. Marion was a single mother. That was the last thing I wanted—for sure. Marion was madcap. I was "too bloody serious".

The other anxiety I had was that Frank had been involved with another girl in my college and he had not entirely broken up with her when he came in pursuit of me. Could I trust him? His interest in being an actor, like my father, both drew me to him and made me cautious. Was he a healthy version of John? And if he was, was that why Marion thought he was not for me? Was he what she wanted? And he wouldn't even flirt with her.

Avocado

I caved in and broke up with Frank. I didn't even try to work things out with him. But I missed him and then was filled with hatred toward Marion. It was Spring Break, and I had to spend some of the time back in her apartment. One day I was alone there, pacing its length and muttering, "Who is she to tell me who is the right or wrong man; she with her dozens of boyfriends, her two ridiculous husbands, and her married lover? Every relationship she ever had at best fizzled out or else ended in disaster." But I wouldn't or couldn't say it to her.

I spied her avocado plant, precariously tilting on three toothpicks in a water glass. She had raised it from the pit, and now it had a long skinny stem and a few leaves. She was proud of it. I grabbed the glass and plant with both hands and smashed the whole thing onto the kitchen floor. It shattered. But that wasn't enough. Amongst the wet shards of glass, I fished out the long stem then snapped it in two. After a very brief moment of remorse, I cleaned up the mess. Then furious again I thought I'd leave just the severed corpse on the kitchen floor for her to find. But I chickened out and threw it all down the smoky incinerator in the hallway outside the apartment door.

I hated her. She was repulsive. She wore a perfume called Charley that smelled all right in the bottle, but on her, it nauseated me.

She had tended that plant for months. I snapped it like I was breaking her neck then dumped and burned the body. I was an experienced killer. I had already smashed the Pote/pot.

She didn't miss it at first but then called me at the college dorm. "Do you know what happened to my avocado plant?"

"I broke it when you told me to stop seeing Frank."

"What! You didn't! What did you do with it?"

"I threw it down the incinerator."

"Oh no! You didn't! That plant was you. I raised it like I raised you. You had no right to destroy it." I was silent.

"No", I thought. "You don't own me—and you didn't raise me, Mama did. And you wouldn't know a good man if you tripped over him." I also could have said, "We are broken." But I said none of it. I had loved her once. That didn't die when I murdered her. And now I hated her with the same passion that I once loved her. Now she was repulsive. She sometimes tried to hug and cuddle me, and I pulled away. She didn't treat me like a daughter, and she didn't treat me like a friend. I sometimes thought, "She confuses me with her lovers. When they aren't around, she wants to hug and kiss me." Whatever it was, I didn't want her to touch me. She noticed it and categorized me as, "…one of those people who don't like to be touched." She was wrong. This was not about me as "one of those people". This was about my hatred of her.

We never repaired things after the avocado. Sometimes, when alone and furious with her, I typed out every kind of crude name I could come up with, bitch, slut, cunt, and twat over and over again. When done I took the pages and ripped them over and over until they were tiny flakes. It did not bring relief.

Better times were friendly but superficial. Worse times I roiled in angry silence. I was always, to the end of her life, afraid I could destroy her with angry words.

Right after she split up with her husband Irv when she turned to me saying, "Let's turn on the gas and die." I knew she was a brittle china doll. You can't play rough with a china doll.

1958: Harry

It is late September 1958 on the campus of Sarah Lawrence College. My friend Jean and I are leaving a dance rehearsal and going back to the dorm when she says, "Would you like to meet someone." "Sure," I say, "Who is he?" "His name is Harry. I worked at his parents' day camp and dated his younger brother Bill a few times. I would love to see more of Bill. But I think you and Harry would like each other. And maybe you and Harry and Bill and I could double date. If he calls and you come to New Haven you can stay with my parents." She goes on saying that Harry left his home city, New Haven, to go to college. Then, after a stint in the army, he is back in New Haven at The Yale Law School. Then pausing first she adds, "But be careful he is a heartbreaker."

If I asked her more about her "heartbreaker" comment, I don't remember what she said. But one thing I did know about myself was that I was cautious to excess and had plenty of experience breaking off relationships before I felt too attached. I began to have some friends, but I was not too close to anyone. I was leading a very busy, independent but not isolated life. And then I met Harry.

Very soon after Jean said she would give Harry my phone number, he called. He was clearly nervous on the phone.

205

"Jean told me that you're a dancer too. Would you like to come to the football game this weekend? Yale is playing Cornell. After there will be a party at my friend's house and then there is a dance that evening at the Law School. If you could come to New Haven by noon, I can pick you up at the New Haven train station. I'll have my parents' car."

"Sounds ok", I say, "but I can't possibly arrive by noon. I have a rehearsal all that morning."

We agree I'll arrive around 2:00 and we'll skip the game. I was delighted to skip the game. I had no interest in football and only later remembered that it was Cornell playing Yale when our son went to Cornell and Harry reminded me.

On the train, I argue with myself, "Why am I chasing all the way to New Haven? Am I so hard up for a date? I could have gone into New York for the afternoon and gone to the new exhibit at MoMA or worked on a paper that's due for school. This is a waste of time!" The conductor calls, "New Haven, last stop."

The train pulls into the station. I get off and there's no one there. Then I look toward the stairway. Up from the station, out of the stairwell and onto the platform, a smiling young man with an easy loping gait runs towards me. He is broad shouldered and slim but sturdy with thick auburn hair the color of burnt sienna. He wears khaki pants and a crew neck sweater the same color as his hair. His smile is very broad.

"Hi, I'm Harry." He seems to automatically know I am the girl he is supposed to meet on the train platform. A barrage of questions follows. "How was the train ride? Did your rehearsal go well? When is the performance? What is it is like to live in New York? What are you majoring in?"

He goes on and on. I feel almost badgered with his questions. Is he really that interested? Is he just nervous? We have just barely entered his parents' car. Then he says, "We're not due at the party until after 5:00.

Would you like to have a tour of New Haven?" We set out through different neighborhoods. He knows the city very well. He tells me he grew up here and then worked for the mayor for several months after college, before going into the army reserves. His mother had been a schoolteacher then spent many years as an Alderwoman. His father is the principal of a public elementary school. Yes, he has a brother Bill who is now a junior in college and planning to go to medical school and his sister Ruth, the youngest, is in high school. Then he says, "Would you like to get the best view of the city?" New Haven nestles between two enormous rock formations, West Rock and East Rock. We drive up to East Rock where the whole panorama stretches in front of us. At the top of East Rock, I stand near the edge of the barrier and he says to me, "Some people get frightened of the height up here. As a dancer, you probably have good balance."

There is still time before the party. He suggests we go to his parents' home and say hello to them. I think to myself, "He must be running out of things to do with me before the next scheduled event."

On the way, in the car, I look over at Harry's profile. He has a perfectly shaped head, His thick hair fits him like a helmet, and he has a strong Roman nose. Suddenly I find him extraordinarily attractive. In profile, he looks somewhat like Erick Hawkins my first male dance teacher.

We meet his mother and father. They are both warm and welcoming although I think a little surprised that Harry has stopped by and introduced me. Do they know this is our first date? Do they know we met only an hour and a half ago?

They ask the standard questions about school and where I am from. Ruth, his sister, is also at home. Ruth, Harry and his father all have the same big, broad smile. Harry looks like his father except that his father has dark eyes and hair and Harry like his mother is fair.

We do go to the party. I can't remember a thing about it. Then he brings me to Jean's house where I will stay that night. I change to go to the dance, and off we go to the Law School.

The band is playing, and we dance. We dance together as though we have danced together for years. We don't speak. Our bodies are in sync. He moves close , and I feel completely held and filled with desire. This is new. I feel desire and comfort and safety at the same time. As a dancer, I loved dancing with a partner and being lifted. It was dramatic and demanded mastery of weight and counter-weight and always the exciting risk of defying the pull of gravity and injury. But this was different. This was melding, mingling, merging.

The band takes an intermission. Harry points to the main door of the hall and says, "Do you see that couple coming through the door now?" I look and see an attractive young woman and man. Then Harry says, "I have a date with her next week. But can I see you again the week after that?" This was the moment that changed the rest of my life.

Over the years we have told friends about that moment, and usually, they have been horrified by what Harry did. They seem to think that pointing out the pretty girl he is planning to see next week and asking me to wait for him goes counter to acceptable courtship behavior. I had the opposite reaction. His honesty completely took me. I was amazed that he was not going to dump her to see me sooner. It was clear that she was not a steady girlfriend since she was coming to the dance with someone else. Harry was going to show up for her. And then he wanted to show up for me. He wasn't playing coy games. His talk was real talk. And he was confident I would wait for him.

After the dance, he took me back to Jean's house and said he would come by in the morning. We may have kissed goodnight. I certainly would have been willing to. He showed up early the next morning. We had breakfast together, took a long walk and then he drove me to the train station. When I arrived back at school, I called Marion and said to her, "I met the man I'm going to marry?" I don't remember what she said or asked, maybe something like, "Ohhh?"

Harry soon called, and we planned to meet in New York for the day. The French Theater was in town, and he suggested we go. I think this was our only insincere moment. Neither of us was interested in seeing an 18th-century play in French, but I suspect we were trying to impress one another. "Yes, I would love to." I said. He bought tickets and we suffered through it together and laughed about it for years.

We continued to see each other most weekends. He either came to Sarah Lawrence or I went to New Haven and stayed overnight at his parents' home. If I went to New Haven by train he usually drove me back to college Sunday night and then, very late at night drove back alone to New Haven. I told him I didn't mind taking the train back. "I want to drive you." he objected, "It gives us more time together."

A few weeks later, after phoning Marion to announce that I would be coming to the apartment, I brought Harry to meet her. She asked him the usual questions about school and future career plans. He did not linger in conversation with her. She turned on the charm admiring his Ivy League credentials. He was, perhaps too obviously, immune to her coyness.

During that first meeting with Marion, he perched himself on the arm of the sofa, clearly not settling in for an extended conversation with her. I stood next to him pleasurably taking full notice of his very broad shoulders under his well-fitting blue blazer. I slipped my arm across the full width of that gorgeous landscape. These were shoulders that could carry a lot and in front of Marion, I staked my claim. Harry and Marion did not like each other, and both let me know it.

On another visit to Marion's place, Walter was present. Harry and Walter drifted into a political discussion, and soon Walter said to Harry,

"Harry, that is where you and I part company." Inevitably Marion soon said, "He is not for you. He's an arrogant snob." Harry was not an arrogant snob, but he had very strong opinions. In his excitable youth, the force of his ideas could take precedence over pacifying any of his interlocutors.

Harry came from a world that I had witnessed desirously and from a distance in the homes of some of my friends. It was the lifestyle that I imagined Sean offered to Marion and that she had refused. Harry's parents, long-married schoolteachers, were involved in their communities and devoted to their three children. Did Marion, twice divorced, now feel on the fringe? She continued to press me to stop seeing him. I caved in. It was not the same as when I caved into her dislike of Frank. I had my own doubts about Frank. I think with Harry the intensity of my attachment to him and my passionate excitement frightened me. I told myself, "Too much—too fast." I told him, "Things feel too intense too soon. I need a break."

Showing Up

Junior year, I tried to imagine the future after graduation. I knew I never again wanted to live with Marion. If things did not work out with Harry, I needed an alternate plan, an ace in the hole. A senior I knew at Sarah Lawrence, an actor, applied for and received a grant to study mime with Marcel Marceau in Paris. It intrigued me. It might bring me back to dance but in a different way. I had mentioned it in passing to Harry.

When I told him, "I needed a break." We didn't see or talk to each other for a month. I spent the Christmas vacation with Marion. One night on returning to the apartment I found a stack of books with labels from the Yale Library. There was no note, just the books. They were on Mime.

Of course, I called him, and we flew to each other with even more passion and yearning than before. He understood that I needed him to pursue me and to show up. He proved he really wanted to be with me and yet also gave me the freedom to say no and yes. We were soon engaged. We had decided not to get a ring because of the expense. But then one night as we were hugging each other in one of the little New York parks that border the East River, a park I had played in as a child,

Harry slipped a ring on my finger. It was an engagement ring with a tiny diamond. His sister had given it to him after she had recently inherited it from their grandmother. I was certainly going to marry Harry, and he came with the gift of his whole family. His sister and I became, and still are, very close. I let go of the plan to go to Paris.

During our engagement, we planned to get together every other week and on our off weeks do as much schoolwork as we could so that our times together would be freer. It didn't work. Harry often just showed up on the off weeks. So we tried to have study time together. Sometimes it even worked.

We planned a small, modest wedding to take place the week after I graduated from college. A friend of Marion who lived outside the City offered her home for the ceremony and reception. Harry's family Rabbi agreed to officiate. Marion and I were drawing up the guest list. We, of course, invited Natalia, Mama, Lenny, and Gloria. Harry invited his relatives. And we included some friends. Then Marion said, "And of course Walter will be there." She had already told me that she planned to break up with Walter because he was making no effort to leave his wife. "No!" I objected. "This is Harry's and my wedding. I don't want your married lover there. You're planning to leave him anyway and he doesn't even like Harry or me." I imagined one of his children bursting into the wedding and making a scene.

Marion was furious and shouted, "Who do you think pays your tuition?" I was shocked. At that moment I could only think she was making herself into a whore and expecting me to be grateful for it. It was Marion who pushed for Sarah Lawrence. I expected to go to one of the City Colleges. I was already admitted to Hunter College where I knew I could get an excellent education. But Marion told me I could apply to Sarah Lawrence. I knew Sarah Lawrence would give me the opportunity to hold onto dance, perhaps return to it later and also take a break from the New York scene. I could also study choreography there, and it was a clear chance to move away from Marion.

I had a partial scholarship as well as a loan, and I earned spending money by babysitting and waitressing. I thought Marion was managing to pay the remainder of the tuition. Suddenly I was told Walter was paying the remainder. I knew Walter gave Marion expensive gifts. He also provided her with a lifestyle she enjoyed—theatre, vacations, and fancy restaurants. Did Walter's wealth and the wealthy appearance of having a daughter go to an expensive college bind her to him? Did she ever love him?

Maybe he loved her, and that is what she needed. Sometimes she called herself a "kept woman." I suspect she was sick of being poor. I would soon graduate from college. Soon she wouldn't need his money for that. Was that why she was ready to leave him? Maybe she did think she was providing me with something I wanted. But I certainly didn't want her to be a lover to someone she didn't want only to get me through college.

And only now, with the perspective of so many decades after can I imagine that with her daughter getting married Marion also wanted to believe that she too was part of a couple. But Walter was not her husband or fiancé or her domestic partner. He had his wife and family, and he was not about to leave them for her. At the wedding, how would he introduce himself? If he came, it could only be a charade. But at least she had the imagination to want something she didn't have. Mama could not even allow herself to want.

I cannot wrap my mind around Marion's strengths without seeing her weakness. I can't think of her as weak without also acknowledging her determination and liveliness. I can't see her selfishness and lack of empathy without also seeing her good intentions, misguided at times. She was no model for loving someone yet she desperately wanted to be loved. She was a mosaic or a collage of shifting personas. It has taken a lifetime to see that more clearly.

Walter did not come to the wedding, but not because of any decision. Within weeks after Marion told me about his paying my tuition, she received a phone call from a colleague of his who either knew about or learned about Marion. He told her that while having lunch at his club that day, Walter had a massive heart attack and died immediately. She called me at school to tell me. Marion was distraught but said she was relieved she had not yet told him she wanted to break-up. Then she added, "It was gentlemanly of him to die like that. He saved me from rejecting him."

After her call, I went right to her apartment. I had visions of her threatening suicide as she had done after Irv left. She said she felt desperately alone. Walter just disappeared. She couldn't go to the funeral. She could talk to one or two friends, but none of her friends knew Walter. Around nine o'clock the same night I called Harry to tell him about Walter and also to tell him I would stay in the City with Marion for a while, maybe for a week. Harry said he would keep in touch. Two hours later the doorbell rang. Harry showed up.

The next day the obituary appeared in the paper with the name of the funeral home. Harry called the funeral home to ask when might be a good time for a private visit. At the suggested time the three of us took a cab downtown to view the closed, heavily carved, mahogany casket. Marion was grateful to Harry but still she never fully accepted him.

For sure, Harry and I were two besotted, crazy-in-love kids. But his showing up to help Marion through Walter's death and to help me with Marion was a revelation of his fine character at a new level.

I loved him. I desired him. I admired and respected him. But could I believe it? Was my life real? Could I relax into it and fully believe what I had in this fine man? He was the finest man I knew, graceful in body, mind, and character and he also loved me. I don't think Harry thought of himself as rescuing me, but I felt rescued from the scattered, unpredictable, shards of my family. Why wasn't he more cautious about getting involved with someone from such an unstable background, so different from his own? Suddenly, loving him as I did felt dangerously risky. I could lose him. He could fall in love with someone else. He could see that I was not right for him. He could die.

During the years in college my fear that Marion could die or disappear gradually faded then disappeared. I could be on my own. The price of that respite was to avoid getting close to anyone. But now, with Harry, I was in deep.

"I Thought All Brides Cried."

O ur life together began in a small rented apartment in the attic of a two-family house, furnished with second-hand furniture from a departing graduate student. Harry continued as a law student. I needed to find a job to support us. There was teacher shortage at the time, and temporary permits were available for college graduates. I found a job teaching first grade in a public school in a nearby industrial town, Naugatuck, Connecticut, home of U.S. Rubber and Naugahyde, synthetic leather used as coverings for furniture, especially diner booths.

The first graders were eager and often bright from very large, economically poor families. I was lucky to get the job. The likely alternative was to be stuck in some office doing mind-numbing clerical work. But I knew nothing about teaching first grade. The kids bore with me, and I think all of us improvised and many even learned to read, probably in spite of me rather than because of me.

Teaching first grade continued for two years while Harry finished Law school with an additional degree in American Studies. He was interested in civil rights, possibly politics and social and economic development of cities

Along with the challenge of teaching, another early challenge was learning to drive a car. The only cars I ever rode in were those belonging to boyfriends, Marion's or mine. I never gave a thought to driving a car. But now I had to drive to work and to most other places around where we lived. Driving a car felt like driving a bomb. For me, it was a not so well guided missile that could kill or maim people both outside and inside the car. Harry drove me to the original interviews. Then I took driving lessons and managed to get my license the week before school began. The Sunday before I asked Harry to come for a rehearsal drive to Naugatuck.

We set out, and as we were about to enter the town, we drove to the top of a very steep hill. Reaching the summit, I looked down what to me was an almost vertical, winding road and panicked. I wailed, "I can't do it. I'll kill someone. I'll kill us both. You'll have to divorce me. I can't support us. It is too much for me. I'm a coward!" Harry stayed calm. In a commanding voice, he said, "You can do this!' After a few more frantic whimpers I shifted into low gear, it was a shift car, and like a cowardly caterpillar slowly inched down the hill. We stayed married. I managed to get through those years on the road even through ice and snow, but never easily.

Weekdays for us were filled with the routines of studying and working. I also imitated Harry's mother as she performed her wifely duties, shopping, cooking, cleaning, washing, ironing, and even mending. Saturdays I did other errands and prepared for school for the following week. On Sundays, I cried. I had no idea why I cried. I was so lucky! I loved Harry, and he loved me. His family embraced me. But if he was late coming home, I panicked just as I had done as a child with Marion. I feared I would never see him again. If he walked home from Law School, he could get caught in the crossfire of rival gangs. He could fall deathly ill. He could die in a car crash.

I began to have a repeating dream of driving a car, and suddenly I hit and kill a man. I had already thought of my encounter with my father just before Harry, and I married as "a hit and run." I had stunned John with a sudden call out of nowhere and just as suddenly rejected him. Wasn't that a kind of hit and run? I began to guiltily ruminate about all those years I had said he was dead. Wasn't the fear and threat of losing Harry justifiable punishment?

Another disturbing dream lingers in memory. I am walking up the red-carpeted stairs of Radio City Music Hall in all its gaudy red and gold excess. At the top of the stairs, I see John. He is wearing a huge sequined, pink cloak in the style of Liberace. He looks at me and in an affected voice oozing with sexuality calls out "Fabulous, fantastic, marvelous". I awake feeling repelled and frightened by his seductive and ludicrous theatricality.

Was John's maudlin, drunken state when we met and my fear that he was confusing me with my mother behind this dream? Even though Natalia had not yet told me about finding him in bed with a man the dream feminized him to excess to look like a cartoon of Liberace. Was I ridiculing him?

In spite of loving Harry and his frequent displays of loving me, I was depressed. Was I finally allowed to feel some of the sadness and confusion of growing up? But I also felt deeply inadequate. Harry's friends and fellow students were formidably smart and accomplished. They were informed about the world and spoke with each other at a level I barely understood let alone could keep up with. Social events, with their high-level academic talk, were a torment and not infrequently I retreated to an empty room or even the bathroom where I curled up and cried.

How did Harry as a young and newly married man stand it? How did he tolerate his tearful, nervous wife? I was convinced it was only a matter of time before he gave up on me. But he didn't. On Sundays when I was inconsolable, he usually said, "let's go for a ride." and we took long rides often into the hilly Connecticut countryside. He over and over reassured me that he wanted to be with me. Years later when I asked him how, as still a young person himself, he bore my neediness and sadness. He replied, "It was easy. I loved you, and I thought all brides cried."

When Harry finished school, I went to the Columbia School of Social Work intending to become a psychotherapist. After, I found a job working in a Child Guidance Clinic with a marvelously talented and supportive staff. I loved the work. People were passionately interested in the experience of children, especially troubled children. We all worked with both the parents and the children. I was younger than many of the parents that I saw in therapy. Many asked me if I had children and when I said, "Not yet." they told me that I couldn't possibly understand what it was like to be a parent. I think they were right, but I could understand what it meant to be a troubled child.

1964: Thank-you But No Thank-You

Tentatively, I still held onto dance. I took local dance classes in New Haven. Also, every summer The Connecticut Dance Festival was held at Connecticut College. Top New York choreographers and performers came for six weeks to perform and to teach. In 1964, using my summer vacation time, I commuted daily to Connecticut College to take two or three classes a day. I wanted to see if I could regain my technique. By the end of the summer session, one of the choreographers who I had worked with in New York said, "You haven't lost much."

That winter, a New Haven choreographer invited me to perform in a play with a long dance sequence at New Haven's Long Wharf Theatre, an equity repertory company. It was tempting at first. It could be a road back to dance. I gave it a lot of thought. Memories of long night and weekend rehearsals flooded back. I knew Harry would never tell me not to do it. But did I want it? Dance as a teenager gave me the freedom to move away from my family and move on with a life of my own. Dance no longer felt like freedom. Life with Harry and with my new work as a psychotherapist was the life I knew I wanted. While I knew I wanted it, and I had it, it didn't yet feel real. Was I pretending? Was I on stage playing a part? How could I possibly have a real life so different from the three generations of women who preceded me? Did it make any sense to try to dance again? Would I be going back to an old life I knew just to escape the strangeness of normality? I was like a refugee who arrives in a new safe country, but it doesn't yet feel like home.

But when I finally said to the choreographer "Thank-you for offering me the part but I'm leaving dance." to my surprise, it felt right and real. The crucial importance of movement of body and mind felt permanent and went back to running in the Sheep Meadow. But being a dancer was now past. Like loving Marion when I most needed to, I loved dance when I most needed it. Without either, I might have suffered some kind of emotional collapse. I wanted to move on—to move to a new home. I was ready to give up being a refugee for being an immigrant. It would take some time to become a citizen in this new country I called *Normal*.

Marion Marries

At age fifty, Marion feared her options to find a man to marry would soon diminish, and so she hurriedly married her last husband, Caleb. Caleb was a consultant at the company where she worked. His wife had recently died, and he too was desperate to re-marry. He had no children or siblings and no other close family. He courted Marion and within a month proposed to her, wooing her with the promise that as long as he lived she would be his treasure and he would "carry her around on a velvet cushion." They were married in New York's City Hall two months after meeting. Harry and I were their witnesses and the only people in attendance.

Caleb took good care of Marion and treated her as a treasure—his treasure. The price for her was to tacitly agree that he was the only important person in her life and in return she would be the only important person in his life. Finally, she found a man who wanted only her. He controlled her, shaping her political, religious and social ideas to be as conservative as his own. She obliged, devoting herself to him. She was now his china doll. He wanted to spend all his free time alone with her. At first, she thought she might like to work part-time, perhaps in a little gift or clothing shop. He discouraged it. He saw to it that she was dependent upon him. But unlike her former husbands, he took excellent care of her, and the marriage lasted.

They moved to Maryland, where, until he retired, he worked at a branch of his company. They made a few acquaintances, their financial advisor and a neighbor or two but they did not socialize much. They watched movies, went to local theater performances, took some short trips, played cards and Caleb drank, but to his credit, he stopped when Marion said she wanted him to. Marion again took up some of her needlework. Caleb kept his promise. He did not abandon his Marion. And Marion devoted herself to him.

He tolerated occasional visits with Harry and me, but as our children grew from being cute lap babies into children with minds and personalities of their own he did not hide his dislike of them, and Marion followed right along. Marion complained our children ignored her. She did not reach out to them but expected them to be interested in her. They tried to call her "Grandma" and Caleb "Grandpa" which is what they called Harry's parents. Marion wanted to be called "Grand Mare " which they didn't quite do and ended up calling them "Marion" and "Caleb."

When Marion gave them gifts she thought they wanted, she complained that they did not appreciate them. A gift to Sarah, age seven, was an old fashioned doll Marion made from a kit. She told Sarah not to play with it but to put it on a shelf as a decoration. One of her gifts to Matthew I returned to her. It was an antique bank portraying a sadistic looking white dentist pulling the tooth of a cartoonish looking black child. She certainly knew better but was so brainwashed by Caleb's values she couldn't understand my distaste for the racist toy. She felt insulted and called us "Northeastern snobs." It was especially puzzling because she had provided me as a child with toys I really loved like Tinker Toys, books, records, Lincoln Logs, a dollhouse, and art supplies. She now belonged to Caleb and included only Caleb in her world.

Eventually, there were no gifts for Matthew and Sarah, not even birthday cards. This was notable because Marion and Matthew shared the same birthday. Most upsetting to me was her lack of any curiosity or interest in Matthew or Sarah.

Marion's rejection of my family was the breaking point for me. I no longer felt any affection for her. At best I tolerated her during our more and more occasional contacts. Whenever I left a visit or hung up the phone, I felt empty and sad, sad that my mother dismissed the life that I treasured. It was a new edition of her abandonment.

However, I did find one path to keep a connection to her. When I began psychoanalytic training and my personal analysis, I asked Marion many questions about her early life, about Mama, Natalia, and Lenny and about her time with John. She was interested in talking about all this history. I never asked about John's sexual interest in other men, even after Natalia told me about it. Marion never mentioned it. It was either unspeakable or maybe, conveniently forgotten.

Why didn't I bring it up? I wanted to hear all that she was willing to say. I didn't want to risk stopping that flow. I was grateful that we could talk about something real. I also didn't want to raise it and have her deny it or say it was a figment of Natalia's crazy imagination. I wanted John's attraction to men to be true, because if it was true, I could understand him, living at his time, as a suffering man. It makes his abandonment of me more bearable. Now I wonder if I had raised it with Marion, would she have opened up more? Or if she denied it, I could still suspect it was true.

Caleb soon made it clear to Marion that if he predeceased her, she was not to leave any money to her grandchildren. He died at age 91. She would die two years later at age 92. They were married for almost forty years. I will never know what she might have been like in her later years if she had not been with Caleb. I suspect she would have taken on the required persona of whomever she was with. At least Caleb took good care of her. Harry and I were grateful for that.

1971: The Dream

Alone, I stand on a high balcony suspended over a vast library with soaring vaulted ceilings. Far below I see large mahogany tables illuminated by green-shaded reading lamps. People bend over their books. I look closely at the balcony where I stand precariously—it is very small and low, made only of papier-mâché. The balcony is a stage set, a prop, extremely precarious but located in a huge library, a space of solidity and import. The balcony begins to crack, then breaks apart. I am falling, about to crash to the marble floor below. I wake with a start.

The dream scene is a combination of the Yale Sterling Library reading room, a scene from current life and the main branch of the New York Public Library reading room, a scene from childhood.

1971: "If We Met for the First Time..."

It took me many years to believe my life with Harry was real. Was it only a dream of what I wished for—not my life? Was I a character in a play pretending I could be married to a solid and fine man? Was I no more than a stage set, made of insubstantial papier-mâché? Had I made myself into what looked like a whole Pote/pot but appearances hid an inner void. Without Harry, the façade would crack, and there would be nothing. I had no substance of my own. It was only a matter of time when Harry would see that he had made a mistake marrying me.

When we were married for eleven years, our marriage hit a major crisis. It began when Harry was suddenly under terrible pressure at work. He did not talk about it. He was distracted and he withdrew from me. This happened from time to time but never for as long or as completely. The children were one and four. Ages one to four were the most turbulent time of my childhood. My parents' separation, many moves, The Green Grass School, and confusion about who was my mother all occurred during those years. That old swampy sub-terrain was now leaking upward into the spaces of Harry's emotional absence. I was panicky and convinced I was alone like the single mothers in the generations before me. I was sure he was getting ready to leave. Did he have someone else? I knew my reaction was exaggerated and far out of proportion to the actual situation but I was terrified. It was so frightening that I had little empathy for Harry or even curiosity about his difficulties. I did not pursue him to ask what was distracting him so. I was afraid of the answer and could only narrowly assume it had to do with me. He wanted to get rid of me. Finally, it's happened. He doesn't love me. I knew it. He wants me out of his life. I was at home full time with the children, not working and seemed to have utterly lost the brief period of self-possession I had as a young dancer and more recently as a young clinician. Angry, lonely and also depressed, I was not unlike Mama when she took care of me. I was suicidal, preoccupied with planning my death. I decided I could go to the shore of Long Island Sound, take all the pills I had, drink vodka and walk into the water.

Suicide as an ace in the hole didn't suffice this time. Life without Harry's love was life without oxygen. But memories of Marion's threats to kill herself rose up, and I knew I couldn't do that to Matthew and Sarah. Next, I decided to run headlong into the very thing I feared most—I would be active, not passive. I would break this spell of terror that he would leave me. Instead, I would leave him telling him we could share custody of the kids. I would go back to work. I would get divorced. Maybe I could find someone new. But could I?

Looking back I am shocked at what I did next. I was not thinking straight. Before I told Harry anything, I called Marion to tell her I was going to tell Harry that I wanted a divorce. She was immediately supportive, more supportive than she had been since my early teen years. She told me she would be available to me; that I must have excellent reasons to feel the way I dd. She asked little about why and said nothing to challenge my decision.

Only in retrospect do I imagine that my terror about Harry's withdrawal and my hell-bent intent to be on my own had at least as much to do with feeling abandoned by Marion as it did about fearing Harry no longer loved me. Talking divorce was speaking her language. She was with me on this. She would be there for me because if I were divorced, I would be like her.

Finally, I angrily confronted Harry. "You ignore me. You don't love me anymore. We ought to separate and probably get a divorce." Fury gave me a brief illusion of control that was about as solid as that papier-mâché dream balcony. But my fury and threat created a counter crisis that shook him. It was as though he woke from his distracted state. He cried. He acknowledged his pre-occupation and spoke about it in detail. Then he paused and looking at me closely said, "No, there is no reason for us to separate. If we met for the first time two years from now, we would fall in love again." He showed up. It was the most present, most healing statement he could have possibly made. It turned things around for me. In it, he acknowledged that there was indeed a new distance between us. He didn't pretend there wasn't. But he intuited that we loved loving each other and he could imagine the future. We would fall in love again. He was wrong about one thing. It took less than two years to re-find each other but with a new difference. Having faced the possibility that I could imagine life without him, as a divorced woman, not only as a dead woman, I never again felt the same desperation that I could not survive without him. I wanted to be with him, but if I couldn't, I would feel wretched for a while and then move on.

But just as compelling was that I recognized I was pretending to be much more substantial than I was. The papier-mâché balcony was a real message. I was haunted by the frightening times and instability of my childhood and teen years. My extreme reaction to Harry's distraction, seeking comfort from my mother, seriously planning how to kill myself, knowing the horrible impact of that on our children, drove me into psychotherapy. Psychotherapy proved immensely valuable. Slowly and carefully I began to build a separate life of my own with Harry. I did some solo traveling. Managing alone in foreign countries was reassuring that I could take care of myself and even have a good time enjoying my own company. It brought back my teenage dancing days in New York where for the first time I believed I could make my own life.

Also, I went back to work, sought additional training in psychotherapy with a plan to eventually begin psychoanalytic training if it became available. I wrote more and having never played an instrument began to study the recorder.

By living a life both separate as well as with Harry, I began to find an inner armature on which to build a sense of core solidity. I suspect the first inkling I had of wanting and needing some inner sense of who I hoped to be was my imaginary boy inside—Marc, the wiry, strong, resilient good sport.

Harry was a wiry, strong, resilient good sport. But unlike Marc, Harry and I were very different. We had different interests and of course vastly different histories. Like Marc, Harry felt it was his business to show up and to help out, so he was also familiar. In this way, Harry lived in my imagination long before I met him. (Is this why people fall in love at first sight?) While he supported me as I built a sense of internal solidity, it was psychotherapy and later psychoanalysis that helped me to believe what we had created together and separately was real.

We began to spend social time with the parents of our children's friends as well as with some colleagues, and in this way developed our life long circle of friends who are now as close as family.

Inventing Marc played an essential part in falling in love with Harry, but it created some problems as well. I attributed too much of Marc to Harry. Marc, after all, was under my control. I could make Marc eternally optimistic, upbeat and always available to me when I needed him. Of course, Harry was going to disappoint me—it was inevitable. By making Harry into Marc, I left Harry too little room for his anxieties and frailties and the times he needed to withdraw and turn inward. As I began to feel more of my strength I could give Harry more room to turn away or turn inward when he needed to. But I could never quite shake the fear that he could abandon me. The fear faded but never entirely disappeared. It was the fault line I brought to the marriage.

In many ways, I consider our life together extraordinary in ordinary ways. We did not do especially exotic things or accomplish fame or fortune, but we loved each other, our children, our work and our friends. Such a life is not without risk. Loving risks loss but it also creates hope, hope to live on.

2005: Marion's End

After Caleb died in 2003, Marion and I were more in touch, and I made a point of visiting and calling her. She was fast becoming more physically and mentally frail. I had to see to it, over her protests, that she stop driving. Soon she became even more unable to care for herself and clearly needed full-time care. I tried to bring in helpers, but she rejected them all. I said, probably more harshly than I needed to, "If you don't want people to come to you, then you need to go to a nursing home." She resisted saying she could take care of herself and didn't want to live in an institution. I responded, "You have no choice you have to go." Recognizing my own irritation, I added, "You have some choices. You can choose to be near me in Connecticut or we can find a place near here." To my surprise, she said, "Ok. I'll go." I then suggested a particular place close to our family where Harry's mother had gone. She said, "No. I don't like cold weather, and I wouldn't know anyone except you. I want to be here." Soon I found a place for her, very close to where she had lived. I moved her in. Suddenly I was flooded with images of The Green Grass School, re-experiencing my terrible isolation and wondered if I was retaliating for the times she left me.

And yet she managed to have a good time for the last two years of her life. She became a star patient—more like a "movie star" patient.

She told the staff and residents stories of her glamorous early life in New York. She told them how she frequented famous "clubs" like 21 and The Copacabana. I brought her a bright pink sweatshirt with "Life Styles of the Rich and Famous" emblazoned in silver across the front. She wore it proudly and often. She was not isolated and enjoyed all the admiration she received for her still present allure and charm. She made some friends and even had some flirtations with male patients.

One of the aids told me she liked to help her get dressed because she had nice clothes and still had something of a figure.

I too admired her refusal to be isolated, pathetic and dependent on me. It felt like the lively best of her. As a child, I suffered from her unpredictability and her many absences. She needed to escape. She ran for her life. She could no longer run, but she could be the star of the nursing home. And she was.

I knew I did not want her to come home with me. Imprisoned with my mother felt too close to a repeat of Mama and Natalia or that winter when I was trapped with Mama. I strongly suspect that even if, in a very weak moment, I offered her my care she would have refused. I didn't want to take the slimmest chance she might say "yes". I am relieved that she did not suggest it. I was also relieved she did not want to move close to our family.

This conveys the stark state of things between us

I called her frequently and about every six weeks traveled to visit her in the nursing home. On these trips, I feared I would be in an accident or fall ill, be unable to return home and then die in her captivity.

As she unraveled more, she occasionally would comment on my body or touch me in ways that I found very uncomfortable. Once reaching out and grabbing my stomach she shouted, "You have a flat stomach." I said to her, "I wouldn't grab at your stomach. Why do you think you can grab at mine?" Coyly she responded, "Because you are my little baby."

This moment reminded me of her once quoting Caleb as saying he could not figure me out and found it hard to talk to me. Then she quoted herself as saying to him, "She is just like me. Talk to her like you talk to me." I was either her baby or herself.

More and more she began to confuse me with Natalia especially after Natalia died. However, we had two moments of real talk. She said she found me to be friendlier than I had been, I think she meant friendlier than when Caleb was alive. It seemed like the right moment to tell her that I found her rejection of Harry's and my children very painful and unwarranted. Her response was unusually clear and surprised me. "Caleb was adamant that I could not leave any inheritance to your children, so I can't do that but I will leave something to your grandchildren." She had no relationship at all with her , but she called in her lawyer and did put her unknown great-grandchildren into her will. I believe it was a peace offering. For me, it was another example of her giving over her mind to someone else, in this case, Caleb. It was as far as she was willing to go. It was painful talk, but it was real talk. I knew just where she stood.

The second moment of real talk came when we were filling out a state form for her final directives. There was a section on visitors. "Who would you like to visit you at the end of your life?" Among her small group of acquaintances, several people were disciples of a local fundamentalist Evangelical minister. They made some attempts to bring Marion into the fold, and she did not resist. With only slightly concealed sarcasm I asked her if she would like the minister to visit her. She burst out laughing at my question saying, "No, of course not!"

For that brief moment, I felt I was with the mother I could remember loving. She recognized my irony. I surmised she went along with her disciple friends when she was with them. I hope she was not just going along with me. I wanted to feel for that moment we were kindred spirits.

I saw her two or three times and again, felt repelled by her body and feared she would touch my body as though she, not I was the owner. I knew she wanted more than anything for me to hold and embrace her but I couldn't. I couldn't bear to touch her. I couldn't love her when she most needed me to. Soon after, she died suddenly of a stroke.

I was surprised by how her death struck me. I longed for the mother I once loved and wished I could have loved her at the time of her death. I wish I could have embraced her. But I suspect if I had tried to overcome my disgust and reach out for her, it would have felt false to both of us. Our bodies can't lie.

She had a small funeral attended by her small band of acquaintances. No one spoke. One woman had a beautiful singing voice and sang "Amazing Grace."

At the deaths of Mama, Natalia and Marion, my so-called three mothers, Marion's funeral was the nearest to being a ceremony that acknowledged a life once lived and now ended.

Sometimes now I dream I am trying to contact Marion. I dial what I think is her phone number but it is not her number, or there is no answer. I awake to feel sad but also glad I can let myself want to reach her.

Marion understood how much I wanted to run and took me to the Sheep Meadow. She supported how much I wanted to dance. She didn't leave me with Mama when she married Irv. Perhaps she did understand that I wished for at least the appearance of a normal family. These are my good feelings about her.

Unlike Mama who mastered not wanting, Marion allowed herself to want. By example, this may have given me the freedom to want as well. Wanting more has been a life force.

2009—2018: Harry

In 2009, Harry's voice, always somewhat soft for a man's voice, began to lose volume. It was especially troubling because he was teaching at the time and had to resort to using a microphone even in a seminar. Gradually he stopped swinging his arms when he walked. He no longer danced at parties. His face began to look less expressive. His eyes blinked less often as though he suddenly saw something frightening. He developed a tremor in his jaw and then in his right hand. Finally, he was diagnosed with Parkinson's disease.

Once again he stepped up and grabbed the challenge. He read about Parkinson's, rode a stationary bike daily, took up the piano again after leaving it in childhood and fiercely worked at his tennis game although he switched to playing doubles. He was going to battle this dragon. He knew it could get much worse despite all his efforts and he did not hide out. He explained his symptoms to people who complained about his low voice. With me he spoke about having "a progressive neurological disease." During this period we moved to a continuing care retirement community into an apartment large enough to have our family and friends visit and stay over. He appeared somewhat stable for several years, especially after he began to take medication. But slowly he needed more and more medication to stem the tide of his physical symptoms as well as increasing episodes of confusion. Eventually, the medication barely worked or worked for only an hour or so. He moved more and more slowly. His reaction times were off. It became unsafe for him to drive. We hassled over his continuing to drive. His father had died twenty years earlier as the result of a car crash. I insisted he stop. He reluctantly and angrily agreed to stop. I found his driver's license in the trash all cut up. I put the pieces back together with scotch tape telling him he still needed it as a picture ID. We were both losing him and we both knew it.

Although he was angry about the constraint on his freedom and angry with me for insisting, I never feared he would take the car keys or secretly drive somewhere when I was away. I trusted him.

He resented my hovering and trying to protect him. He would get tense and angry, telling me to back off and then tell me I was right. And I would yell back, "I am right and I hate being right." I tried to keep my mental balance by telling us both, "Whatever I do is going to feel somewhat wrong or very wrong to one of us."

One of the most difficult symptoms was that he lost the ability to show expression in his face. Along with his body stiffness, his feelings were very hard to read unless he explained what he felt. Often he couldn't.

He sank deeper into depression. He went into therapy. He took anti-depressants but the reality of his disease only progressing overrode any intervention. He was without energy and spoke of how someday he might need to escape from his life because he was only going to get sicker and sicker.

Music seemed to comfort him and for a while to sustain him. We went to concerts and to the opera. Harry's beloved piano teacher began to give him easier pieces to play and later played the left hand while he played the right. He still loved his lessons and loved his teacher who effortlessly supported Harry's continuing interest in the face of continuing difficulties.

By early 2018 he had more episodes of confusion. He was getting lost in familiar places, losing his sense of time and short-term memory. But it was still episodic. At times his mind was clear. He began to use a cane and then needed a walker to keep his balance. His blood pressure became very labile—so low he was at risk of fainting, which he did several times, so high he was at risk of having a stroke—which he managed to avoid—as far as we knew.

He had always managed our finances and I began to take it over—with his help briefly, but then it was clear he could no longer focus or concentrate enough to show me and so I sought help from our accountant and financial adviser who knew Harry well. Both reached out. It was like another first trip as a new driver down that precipitous hill fifty-eight years earlier—and again Harry said to me, "You can do this."

He began to fall, even with the walker, especially during the night when he could not sleep and wandered around in our apartment. Time after time he fell, without serious injury but we had to call for help to get him up. We put up a partial bed rail. He accepted every device.

The first time I tried to help him shower I feared we would both end up bloody messes on the bathroom floor. He accepted help from an aid for showering.

Then one early morning at 3:00 am he had a devastating fall. There was a crash and the loudest scream I ever heard. He was using the walker but somehow cornered himself between a wooden table and an oak chair. He fell fracturing three ribs. He was in the worst excruciating pain he ever knew, and we rode in the ambulance to the hospital After some days his pain was managed and he returned to our apartment complex and admitted to its nursing facility permanently. Now he was confined to a wheelchair. We worked out a plan with the nursing facility where I could spring him from nursing care every morning and bring him to the apartment where we spent the day. But sometimes he forgot he was not safe standing up and would impulsively stand up and try to walk. I dared not leave the room. If I moved through the apartment, I wheeled him with me. If I had to go to the bathroom, I demanded a promise from him that he would not try to get up. I feared if he fell on my watch, I would not be able to take him out of the nursing facility for the day. He kept his promises. He slept much of the day. In the evening before I brought him back to the nursing unit, we watched mystery serials. I believe he followed them sometimes and sometimes not.

He was despondent. We hugged a lot. I touched and stroked him continually and constantly thought, "How much longer will I have him?" Can my hand be indelibly imprinted with the feel of his skin, the silkiness of his hair, the muscles of his broad shoulders? Can my arms be imprinted with the sensation of hugging him? Can my nose be filled with his personal fragrance? Can my cheek always feel his cheek against mine? Can my whole body feel imprinted with the pressure of his body on mine? Will I be able to always evoke the feel of his lips on mine? Will I turn toward him in dreams and have him in all his sensual weight and fullness?"

We went on long rides in the car. We could not stop for lunch because it was too risky for him to get out of the car and into the wheelchair and then navigate through an unfamiliar place. Our adventure in the car was to drive someplace with winding roads and deliberately get lost. Then I would turn on the GPS to "Go Home." We both enjoyed it, especially when the New England foliage was aflame before its winter's death.

Pushing him in the wheelchair was a new view of him. I had never spent time studying him from the back just below eye level. He recently had had a very good but closely cut haircut from a local barber that plainly revealed the beautiful shape of his head and his slender neck. I could see the boy.

During these long days, Harry allowed me to take care of him. He needed help with the toilet. He needed help to get cleaned up, and he needed help changing his clothes. I felt blessed to have his trust. While it reminded me of falling in love with our babies, Harry was not a baby. He trusted me with his most private self and I loved him now in a new sadly pleasurable way.

His confusion and depression worsened. During his stay in the nursing facility, he saw many people in semi-vegetative states slumped all day in their wheelchairs. He said he wanted to die soon and asked me how he could. A close friend had told us how he helped his father die by telling him he could voluntarily stop eating and drinking. Harry and I talked about it. He said he wanted to do it soon. I asked him not to leave me out when he made his decision. I wanted to be with him through it all. I found articles about it and read them to him. Then several times together we spoke to his nursing facility internist about it. It is legal in Connecticut as long as at the time of the decision the person is rational. His doctor said he would help out by providing Ativan and morphine and described what to expect in the process.

Harry's mind continued to episodically abandon him. He had occasional hallucinations, seeing figures of people who were not there. But sometimes his mind was still very clear. I asked him if he wanted me to tell him if he was having more episodes of confusion. He said, "Yes, please." Then one day I did tell him. He immediately sat down at the table and in his wobbly handwriting, but for the moment with a lucid mind, he wrote out the following statement. "I am aware that the symptoms of my Parkinson's disease are becoming worse and the doctors I have consulted concur that the disease at this point is going to continue to progress. I now choose to make the decision to voluntarily stop eating and drinking. I realize this will lead to my death." He called his sister and brother to tell them. They were upset but didn't try to dissuade him. "What a loss!" his sister said. His brother, a physician said he understood adding, "I will miss you". We called Matthew and Sarah. They both knew this was coming. They wanted to make sure it was really time for it.

Harry stopped eating and drinking that day. He turned to me and said, "I will miss you." We lay on our bed, cried and held each other. I called his doctor and the head of the nursing unit to tell them about Harry's decision. We brought what he had written. I moved into the nursing facility with him, and the staff pulled my bed right next to his.

He was mostly conscious the first three days although he was getting more and more sleepy. We listened to gentle baroque music and opera arias, music we had often listened to. We danced in the way we often danced after lovemaking—lying face to face, holding hands each with an arm outstretched we rocked in time to the music, hummed and wept.

The first day I suddenly and silently found myself wondering if what we were doing was like an abortion. I have always been fiercely pro-choice, and I support assisted suicide as a humane act when there is mental and physical suffering that will only get worse, destroying the quality of life. But in the face of losing Harry, I suddenly questioned myself. Then, just as I had these thoughts, Harry turned to me saying, "Am I taking a life? Is it ok?" He must have answered his own question because he didn't ask for food or drink then.

The third day was his last day of consciousness.

Ron, our son-in-law, appeared suddenly at the door of Harry's room. Sarah was with him. As a young husband, Ron had been unreliable, and the marriage suffered. In recent years Sarah and Ron seemed more at peace. After years of erratic employment, Ron finally kept his job. Sarah and Ron were both devoted parents and had acquired a steady circle of shared friends. Things appeared better. We always invited Ron to our home, but he only came occasionally.

Ron walked in, pulled a chair close to Harry and began speaking urgently, "Harry, I need to talk to you. I know I created many of those gray hairs on your head. I was not a good young man. I messed up a lot. But Harry you always welcomed me to your home. I didn't always come. That was because I felt so bad about myself and I felt ashamed of what I had done. But Harry, I watched you. And I learned from you. I watched you be a father, and I watched you be a husband, and Harry, you taught me how to be a man. Now I have this beautiful family. Harry, I owe it to you." We were all weeping.

Sarah was present, but she did not know what Ron was going to say. Then Ron shook hands with Harry, hugged both of us and left. Harry, with his ironic wit that I had not heard in so long, sighing said, "Gee, I should have died more often."

Ron told Sarah, he was so glad Harry was awake and aware when he came, and he knew he came in the nick of time.

As the day drew to a close, Harry was confused again and asked, "When do we eat?" I said, "Do you remember you decided not to eat or drink." He nodded and didn't ask for food or drink again. This haunts me. I think if he had food in front of him and I was not there, he would have eaten—simply because he felt hungry. I had taken care of his body for much of the past year, and now I was reminding him to deprive his body. I was depriving his body.

Rationality leaves out a lot. It only appears to be balanced and clear. When faced with something like assisted suicide or abortion, emotions rush in pulling so-called clarity into a riptide. I assisted Harry's suicide. I helped him to abort his life. It is the most difficult thing I have ever done. If necessary, I hope I can count on someone to help me end my life. But I can imagine in the face of it, having the same questions all over

242

again. Rationally I know that if I had not reminded Harry of his decision he possibly would, in confusion and forgetfulness, as well as hunger and thirst, begun eating and drinking and possibly sliding into permanent dementia. The escape door might have closed. I could not stand by and allow him a living death, to lose his personhood, to become little more than a senseless body requiring only maintenance. The nursing unit was filled with these people who were humanely cosseted, gently crooned to, cleaned, fed and maintained. Of course, I can't know the experience of those patients. Perhaps they lived out their bodily lives in richly textured dreams. I doubt it. Many howled or screamed for hours at a time in what I could only imagine was isolated despair. I could not let Harry slip into that Hell. But were those cries what they felt? I can only know how it sounded, and it sounded agonizing.

Day four, five and six Harry had no fully conscious moments. He barely opened his eyes although he turned toward people's voices and even smiled a little when a friend recited some off-color limericks for him. He could no longer swallow his Parkinson's medication, even if it was crushed so he had only the morphine and Ativan. In liquid form, these could be absorbed when dropped into his inner cheek. Sometimes he had tremors and seemed agitated. I placed my open hand on his chest and hoped the heat and pressure of my hand would warm and soothe him. I had my other hand on my chest, and it seemed to calm us both down. This was a technique we used on Matthew and Sarah when they were little.

Harry now looked thinner, and I could feel his breastbone under my hand. Again I tried to imprint its feel into my palm. He was visibly slipping away. On day six his breathing occasionally paused, and he gasped. The doctor saw him and said he believed Harry was no longer aware of himself or others. I woke many times during the nights to feel his breath against my hand. His pulse was becoming erratic. Friends flowed in and out of the room. Our family mostly sat vigil, making sure Harry always had someone with him. On November 24th around 7:00 pm I was alone with him. He gasped intensely several times and then stopped. His lips were cold. I could feel no pulse. I went to the door and called to the nurse who was nearby. She came right in. Listening with her stethoscope to his heart and his pulse, she turned to me saying, "He has passed." Then she put her arms around me and held me. On November 30th Harry would have been eighty-three.

We were alone together when it happened when he gasped his last breath. It was a desperate gasp. I hope he was not aware of it. It was terrifying but also a deep moment of closeness. We had shared so many moments of profound closeness. This was our last.

Matthew and Sarah and their families were in our apartment, and they all came right over. I also called our close friends who live in the same complex, and they also came right over.

Matthew called the funeral home. The funeral director soon came pushing a gurney. He explained he was going to lift Harry's body onto the gurney and into a bag and that we may not want to watch. Matthew immediately said, "I will help you." Our family did not back away. We wanted to bear witness—mostly we did not want to leave Harry alone. I held his body for a moment now enclosed in a blue bag, printed with a Star of David. Matthew went out with the funeral director and helped him to place Harry's body into the limousine. We were with Harry until there was no choice but to let him go.

Harry died on a Saturday night over a Thanksgiving weekend. The funeral was held on Monday morning.

People from every walk of both our lives poured into the Sanctuary of the Temple. There were people who as children attended his parents' day camp where Harry, as an older teenage waterfront counselor, taught them to swim. In came his tennis buddies, fellow students and faculty from his law school, people from all the organizations he served on, his students from over the years, neighbors, our friends, his friends, my friends, Matthew and Sarah's friends, friends of his sister and his brother, his colleagues, my colleagues, his piano teacher and even some of my former patients saw the obituary and showed up. All came to say goodbye, to hear about and to celebrate his life and to support us.

On the way home, trying to take in the support and caring and very presence of all the people who showed up at short notice, I could only compare it to the terrible bleak funerals of Mama and Natalia and of Marion too. So many people bearing witness to Harry's life, to our life and to Harry's death tells me that we created our life and our life is real.

And then the notes and cards poured in. Dozens of people wrote about his beautiful, broad smile, his intelligence, and his sweetness, the first things that struck me on our very first date along with his relaxed, loping gate as he ran towards me on the railroad station platform on that October Saturday in 1958.

After

Matthew and Sarah, in the spirit of their father, show up and step up. They readily offer both emotional and practical support. I feel Harry's presence in both of them. Our grandchildren too keep in touch. Still, the pain of missing Harry's presence is excruciating. I never know when it will come on and when it does it is like a huge black wave hitting with brutal force. I can be walking in the street or in the supermarket, or doing mundane chores in the apartment. Then I run to his closet to grab an armful of his clothes and sobbing into them, wish he could hold me.

Sometimes I envision him when he was robust and energetic and then when he was sick and falling and confused. I dream he is falling. I try to grab his upper arms, as he is about to go down. I wake grabbing my own arms. It is as though we are one body.

It isn't only painful. The outpouring support of friends and family did not stop at the funeral. It is here now and ongoing in my life. We talk, we listen and we cry.

Now it is the first time ever that I live alone. But when I look back, I will never be as alone as I was as a preschooler at the Green Grass School or during that winter confined with Mama in her apartment.

Again, I compare my life to Marion's after her lover Walter died. She could not even show up at his funeral.

Harry is absent, yet I am filled with his presence. Perhaps that is why his physical absence hurts so much. From our first dance at the Yale Law School, we loved one another, body and soul. Throughout our life, we often danced around the house. We might do the tango or the lindy hop in the kitchen. He easily lifted me off the ground or slid into a French dip. If we folded sheets together we each folded our ends lengthwise then each holding the two ends, polka-stepped toward one another.

Days after the funeral I dreamt we were together in an airport, and suddenly I can't find him. I attempt to call him on his cell phone. And then I remember he died and that I terminated his cell phone service. I wake thinking about John Denver singing, "I'm leaving on a jet plane, don't know when I'll be back again, hold me like you'll never let me go." The fact that I hear *John* Denver does not escape me. History, like old geological rock, is surfacing.

Then soon after, I dream that I bend down to kiss Harry who is lying in bed, but my lips touch only water. I try to hug him, but my arms encircle only water. And then a counter-dream follows. Bending down to kiss his forearm I feel his warm skin and the soft hairs against my lips.

And then I remember 1960, that first rehearsal drive together to my new job. We reach the top of a terrifying and precipitously steep hill. I wail, "I can't do this." In his calmest and most commanding voice he says, "You can do this."

With John, my father, I needed to invent a mostly visual image from only a few shards of what I knew of his life—what I came to call his Pote/pot. I tried to imagine him as a more intact vessel but I will never know what was inside him, his inner life, what he thought, felt, feared or what brought him joy.

In contrast, from the beginning Harry was intact. He was a vivid, whole, three-dimensional, flesh and blood living presence. Filled with passions and ideas, he also had a deep sense of the people he knew and loved.

Vigorously in his personal life and in his work he gave shape to the world around him. He was the most courageous person I ever knew. He never backed away from a problem. He could not solve every problem he took on, but he faced up to everything that came his way. He took hold of the clay of his life, his endowments, the people he influenced, and the people who influenced him and molded a life unique to him. He was not a shard. Unlike John who went missing, Harry showed up, he even showed up for his death. But now he is missing. I feel his leaving in my gut, the way I felt when Marion's train pulled out of Penn Station with all my insides hooked onto the caboose—leaving, leaving, leaving until I was emptied out. I worried that I would forget my mother, I didn't—but I have no worry about forgetting Harry. I won't empty out. He gave me an inner sense of solidity. My quest was to believe it. I know Harry and I loved each other and we loved, loving each other. Our life was real.

I am beginning to know his death is real as well. I dream we are riding in a car together in New York. He is driving. I must stop along the way to retrieve something I forgot from a hotel where we stayed. I return to the street, and he has driven off without me. I wake furious with him. What is the matter with him! How could he drive off without me!

My fury is indeed fury, but it is also a cover for feeling devastated and abandoned. No way can such a monumental moment as losing Harry, especially in the context of his deciding to leave his life, escape the shadow of my early abandonments. Once again, rationality is puny compared to the power of a life history and what it leaves behind.

I dream Harry is lying on his deathbed, his face turned away with a painful grimace. Then I dream his face is covered with a Pyrex dish.

I suddenly wake horrified. Pyrex withstands extreme heat. Cremation was another rational decision we made before he died. No modern Jew, no matter how reformed, can choose cremation without at some point thinking of the Holocaust.

I dream Harry is sitting in his favorite chair, wearing my favorite of his shirts, a blue and white plaid of the softest fabric. He does not see or hear me. He is in his own world as he sometimes was. I tell myself, "He is not ignoring you. He died."

I dream he asks me to keep a magazine that came in the mail. The name of the magazine is "Intervention". Harry wants some article on health care policy. (I don't know if such a magazine exists.) But I forget he wants it and I use it to quickly absorb something that has spilled. It is ruined, and I panic. I wake up and tell myself, "It's ok. He died. He doesn't need it anymore." No more interventions are necessary.

I dream we are enjoying some vigorous sex. I feel his skin and the texture of his hair. He is young and very much alive.

Before Harry died I imagined I would feel wretched for a while and then I would be ok. It is different. Every day I feel both wretched and ok, sometimes in sequence and sometimes at once. I can participate in life; even enjoy myself, sometimes even laughing while at the same time I sit beside myself weeping. I miss him yet there is not emptiness. My mind is full of him. All my senses are alive with terrible grief, deep joy and thousands of images. When I have those occasional moments of feeling like I did at The Green Grass School, devastated and abandoned, I will try to remind myself that only at my death will we finally part. Can I really live in this world without him? "Yes," he would say, "You can do this."

Acknowledgments

Harry, his family, our children Matthew and Sarah, their spouses Hilda and Ron, their children, our grandchildren, Gabrielle, Rafael, and Elena are my bedrock. They fill me with their love and my love for them. They all show up. They abide. They make all the difference.

Our oldest friends, who are now more like family, Sandy and Carol Schreiber, Marc and Anne Schwartz, Joe and Susan Saccio, Jesse and Ruth Geller have all shown me by example how to be a couple and how to parent.

Linda Gravenson, who I have known since childhood is a superb writer and editor. She read much of the memoir and with great care brought to it her outstanding literary skills as well as her innate, psychological mindedness. My only regret is that we had to reach old age before becoming importantly close friends.

Sydney Anderson, a child psychoanalyst, and dear colleague and friend read parts of the book and spurred me on as did Rosemary Balsam and Sybil Houlding.

My writing group at the Western New England Institute for Psychoanalysis, David Carlson, Matthew Shaw, Marshall Mandelkern and Stanley Possick were relentlessly encouraging but also, as fine psychoanalysts do, pressed me on to say more and go deeper.

My literary writing group at The Whitney Center, Mary Davis, Deanie Blank, Margaret Mauldon, Karen Kmetzo, Tom Kmetzo, Peter Hunt and Hal Obstler are committed fiction writers, essayists, and poets. All paid the closest attention to content, language, and style.

I want to especially thank Deanie Blank for our nightly walk/talks full of good conversation about life and writing.

My peer supervision group, Deborah Fried, Lisa Marcus and Nancy Olson, three very fine psychoanalysts, and great friends, read or heard about parts of the memoir and added there clinical insights which again helped me to say more and go deeper.

I also want to acknowledge the process of writing itself. It can open channels in the mind less available to thinking and speaking. Writing was also a faithful companion and friend during Harry's long illness and after his death.

Finally, I thank Dr. Arnold Richards and Tamar and Lawrence Schwartz at International Psychoanalytic Books for their support in publishing the book.

CPSIA information can be obtained
at www.ICGtesting.com
Printed in the USA
LVHW040307170622
721514LV00010B/710

9 781949 093322